'HALLS', 'GRANGES'&
'MANORS' AT WORK

No 7801 *Anthony Manor* with the Pwllheli portion of the down 'Cambrian Coast Express' leaving Morfa Mawddach (formerly Barmouth Junction) on 9 August 1963. *T. Boustead*

'HALLS', 'GRANGES'& 'MANORS'AT WORK

MICHAEL RUTHERFORD

GUILD PUBLISHING
LONDON

First published 1985

This edition published 1987
by Book Club Associates
by arrangement with Ian Allan Ltd

Printed in the United Kingdom by
Ian Allan Printing Ltd

Contents

Cover:
'Hall' class locomotive No 4906 *Bradfield Hall* at Torquay in 1928.
From a painting by G. E. Heiron

Rear cover top:
No 6846 *Ruckley Grange* with an up 'E' headcode freight at Teignmouth. *R. C. Riley*

Rear cover bottom:
No 7827 *Lydham Manor* and 7819 *Hinton Manor* on the Festiniog Railway Society special at Ruabon on 20 April 1963. *T. J. Egdington*

Front endpaper:
No 7901 *Doddington Hall* climbing Chipping Campden Bank with an up oil train on 23 November 1963. *R. C. Riley*

Rear endpaper:
No 7818 *Granville Manor* storms up the bank at Tallerddig with the 'Cambrian Coast Express' in May 1964. *C. J. Blay*

Left:
No 4997 *Elton Hall* piloting No 4700 at Exeter in August 1956. *P. Ward*

Introduction

This book is intended as a companion to my *'Castles' and 'Kings' at Work*. As with that volume I have tried not to repeat everything that has been written before on GWR standard two-cylinder locomotives. 'Halls', 'Granges' and 'Manors' are inexorably associated with Churchward's standardisation and this has been covered in the text. I have again used a documentary approach and included writings from official reports and papers where possible. The text therefore covers a wider scope than the title may suggest; the majority of photographs, however, are of these three classes and I would hope that the excellence of many of them will go some way to balance my proclivity for wandering through so many byways in the maze of GWR locomotive history.

It was with some regret that whilst completing this book I learned of the death of Ernie Nutty who had explained to me about the 'Counties' and his part in the design, as well as giving me an insight into the ways of the drawing office and its staff. He will be sorely missed by all who met and talked of Great Western engines with him.

Very many people have given me a great deal of help and encouragement especially P. K. Jones, and also John Trounson, Kenneth Leech, Alan Wild, Colin Jacks and Vic Webster. I have been 'spoilt for choice' as regards photographs and if I have used yet again any pictures that have been published many times before, it is due purely to favouritism on my part. I must thank Ian Allan for the use of their Library and other collections and also the Keeper of the National Railway Museum for access to material held there. Finally, special thanks are due to Dick Riley and John Edgington who put many of their pictures at my disposal.

Michael Rutherford
York 1984

Below:
No 6861 *Crynant Grange* at Abergavenny Junction on 8 September 1952 with the 8.55am Cardiff-Manchester *P. W. Alexander*

I
The Churchward Revolution

There is nothing more difficult to take in hand, more perilous to conduct, or more uncertain in its success, than to take the lead in the introduction of a new order of things, because the innovator has for enemies all those who have done well under the old conditions, and lukewarm defenders in those who may do well under the new.

Machiavelli

But of a good leader, who talks little,
When his work is done, his aim fulfilled,
They will all say, 'We did this ourselves'.

Laotzu

The mixed traffic 'Halls', 'Granges' and 'Manors' of the Great Western Railway were of the same lineage as the standard two-cylinder engines first propounded by G. J. Churchward in a set of six diagrams drawn up in January 1901. Indeed, the prototype 'Hall' was little more than one of Churchward's '29xx' class 4-6-0s rebuilt with smaller wheels, of 6ft diameter. A 5ft 8in 4-6-0 was also part of the original scheme and a diagram was prepared in 1905 as a preliminary to ordering a prototype. For some unknown reason, no such machine was forthcoming and instead a 5ft 8in 2-6-0 appeared in 1911, a tender version of the large boilered standard 2-6-2T, the '3150' class. These versatile 2-6-0s eventually numbered 342, and the renewal of 300 of them as 'Granges' and 'Manors' was planned from 1936, but as we shall see only 80 'Granges and 30 'Manors' were built.

Churchwards' thinking for an enlarged 2-6-0 centred around a 5ft 8in 2-8-0 and following the construction of a prototype with a standard No 1 boiler, which was rebuilt with a larger No 7 a further eight of the class were built. These impressive locomotives were severely restricted as to which routes they could use and their number was never increased.

George Jackson Churchward is rather an enigmatic figure. We have his own words only through a few published papers and his contributions in discussion of the papers of others. He wrote no books and appears to have left no diaries or memoirs; his public image, a bachelor, living in a large house with several servants and interesting himself in motoring, gardening and country pursuits such as fishing and shooting, belies a man of exceptional abilities. No chief mechanical engineer of any British railway company managed the depth, and no Continental equivalent, the breadth of Churchward's professional technical interests; not to mention his main task, which was the management, at the most senior level, of a vast department employing thousands of men (37,000) and dealing with a yearly budget measured in millions of pounds sterling, even before World War I. He claimed that he was lucky in the quality of the men that he gathered around him. This is however *the* main secret of good management and his ability to bring the best out in others and gain their confidence and respect is legendary. No one who ever knew him spoke of him with anything other than affection.

There have been a number of books and papers written of Churchward's locomotive work but none that include the work of his department as a whole; locomotives, carriages, wagons, workshops, locomotive sheds and other outside plant etc.[1] He is thus reduced to a 'locomotive designer' and compared with other 'locomotive designers' at home and abroad. Although then, this book will deal with some of his locomotives and their derivatives, it should be remembered that, like Gooch before him on the GWR, Webb at Crewe on the LNWR and Aspinall at Horwich on the L&YR, he ran a vast and complex empire in which all parts were in some way interlinked.

He can in fact be regarded as a pioneer of the prize baby of the 1970s – Terotechnology. This was described as:
'A combination of engineering, management, financial and other practices applied to physical assets in pursuit of economic life cycle costs.

'It is therefore concerned with the specification, design, provision, installation, commissioning, maintenance modification and replacement of plant machinery, equipment and buildings, and with feedback of information on performance, design and costs.'[2]

General opinion regarding Churchward's locomotive work was well expressed by J. N. Westwood:
'To summarise the Churchward achievement, without being himself especially inventive, he yet caused more of a change in locomotive design than any of the more revolutionary designers. He did this by careful study of what had been done in the past and in other countries. His debt to American practice was substantial; and his espousal of generous steam ports and passages probably came from studying the legendary free-running of Crampton's locomotives. Though not the first to see the importance of liberating the hitherto constricted steam, he was the first to do so in so public and successful a manner that he was widely imitated. He gave the Great Western a standardised locomotive stock that was technically so advanced that his designs were barely outclassed half a century later.'[3]

This is to some extent unintentionally patronising, with the benefit of hindsight (but *is* the general view of many enthusiasts, both amateur and professional). If he made more of a change in locomotive design then he *was* the *most* revolutionary of designers. An engineering revolutionary should not be pictured as a late 20th century political *poseur* . Many highly regarded locomotive 'innovators who followed him produced very expensive and unreliable machinery worthy of a Heath Robinson or Roland Emmett. One of the great railway engineers, Professor Lomonossoff had a rule that he taught his students – as an engineer, do not try to invent, do real design-work; that is try to solve problems by thinking them out on paper as they occur. It is also most unlikely that Churchward knew anything of the work of Crampton's locomotives. The need for large steam passages was known at the beginning of the GWR, indeed it was a condition of Brunel's when ordering the first locomotives, that generous steam passages should be employed. Churchward's interest in American practice was from the production side as much as anything, He wished to standardise parts and mechanise production in areas where highly skilled fitters could be replaced by semi-skilled or unskilled men. It had been a necessity in American industry from the very beginning to develop this approach, because skilled labour was extremely expensive or unobtainable, whereas land and its wealth (wood, coal, ore) was cheap. In England skilled labour was very cheap, but Churchward saw the way the wind was blowing and wished to increase the manufacturing efficiency of Swindon Works at a time when there was a national upsurge in business and commerce (and pleasure activities) and the GWR was beginning a gradual and sustained growth and expansion.

His plain and straightforward long-lap, piston valved machines with long piston stroke and relatively high boiler pressure appeared contemporaneously with various four-cylinder compounds and Schmidt superheated simples in Europe. Due to his own modesty and self-effacement, it is always supposed that Churchward gained a great deal from the Continent – full stop. It is most likely however that any debts were repaid in kind and with interest.

It is uncertain when Churchward's interest in American practice first began; his enthusiasm was not universally shared in England. A paper was read to the Institution of Civil Engineers on 31 March 1903 by P. J. Cowan and entitled *American Locomotive Practice*. A Mr Lart made his views *very* clear in the discussion which followed. He thought:

'The Paper would do good in exposing the fallacy, deeply rooted in some minds, that American methods (not only in regard to locomotives, but also to other things) were so superior to British methods, in theory and in practical results, that they should be adopted wholesale in England and the Colonies, and should supplant, as quickly as might be, the assumedly antiquated system which had served so well since the locomotive was first used in England. In fact, it was difficult to gather from the paper in what particular or general points American locomotive practice could claim to be superior to British. The impression conveyed by the Paper seemed to be that roughness and cheapness were the only ideals aimed at, and that durability and efficiency were not considered at all. The first characteristic was no doubt fully attained; but it was difficult to see where cheapness of first cost or maintenance could come in, when an engine was deliberately built to last only a few years, and then to be bodily scrapped to make way for another, equal in ugliness and complexity, and destined in due course to fall to pieces like its predecessor. American engineers, in fact, were positively proud of such rubbish; but what amount of work they got out of these clumsy machines few people seemed to know.'

He went on in this vein before putting a word in for F. W. Webb's one major professional aberration, his compounds, by that time rejected even by his LNWR colleagues.

Whilst manager of the locomotive works Churchward began to introduce American machinery and he later took on E. A.

Below:
Churchward's original standard engine scheme of January 1901. Only No 100 appeared in this form, the other types had tapered boilers and larger diameter piston valves. The smaller-wheeled 4-6-0 did not emerge until 1936 in the form of the 'Grange' class. *Author's collection*

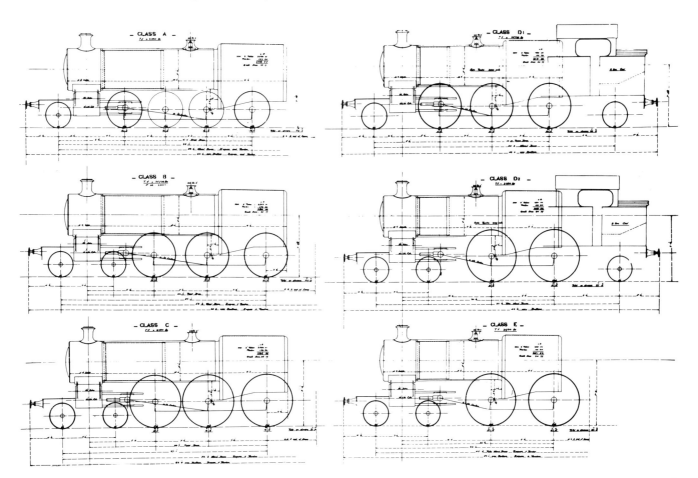

9

Watson, an Irishman by birth (and later CME of the Great Southern & Western Railway) to apply the American methodology that he had learnt at Schenectady (ALCO) and Altoona (Pennsylvania Railroad).

Standardisation

It is a coincidence of some significance that the month of January 1901 should see both Churchward's scheme for standard locomotives drawn up, and the setting up of the Engineering Standards Committee as the result of a motion by Sir John Wolfe Barry at a meeting of the Council of the Institution of Civil Engineers. Initially the object was the comparatively limited one of arranging a series of standard rolled sections of iron and steel. A great percentage of engineering structures, especially bridges, ships and rolling stock, are made up of such rolled material. It would appear that manufacturing delay and a good deal of waste was due to the production of a superfluous multiplicity of different sections made to the needs of different engineers, at different times, and for various purposes. A much smaller number of sections could have met all needs if they could have been selected on some rational system. But it was also clear that an influential and representative authority was necessary, to make a selection of standard sections which would be likely to be generally accepted as sufficient by engineers and manufacturers. The need of systematisation in other branches of engineering soon became obvious; and the work of the committee was extended in very many directions.

Standardisation can be regarded from a number of different points of view, for example: a) Thread forms, limits and fits, rolled sections etc. b) Nuts, bolts, rivets, flanges etc. c) Assemblies and accessories. d) Complete machines. and also whether those standards fall into the following categories: 1) Company standards. 2) Industry standards. 3) National standards. 4) International standards.

The most tireless champion of greater accuracy and precision in engineering matters was Joseph Whitworth who introduced his standard range of screw threads in 1841. To a meeting of the Institute of Mechanical Engineers in 1857 he showed, using accurate gauges, that even a discrepancy of one hundred thousandth of an inch could make all the difference between a driving fit and a loose fit. He asked, 'what exact notion can any man have of such a size as a ''bare sixteenth'' or a ''full thirty-second''?'.

It is a little alarming to read O.V.S. Bulleid who in 1941 said: 'There was a tendency nowadays to talk about thousandths of an inch. He did not like thousandths; he preferred to talk about a sixty-fourth, or half of a sixty-fourth. He liked the Irishman who referred to ''a very small piece, about the back o'my nail''. He understood that kind of engineering, When he heard young men talk about thousandths, he felt that the thing would probably seize, or do something it should not do, whereas when one talked about sixty-fourths it would work.

'He thought it was really a question of applying sheer commonsense to the working of a machine which was not a precision machine. . .'

It is perhaps ironic that 14 years later K. J. Cook, former Works Manager at Swindon and later CM &EE of the Western Region should entitle his Presidential Address to the Institution of Locomotive Engineers as *The Steam Locomotive: A Machine of Precision*. Some years before Bulleid's remarks however,

Swindon was able to erect Churchward's standard locomotives with remarkable accuracy using Zeiss optical equipment, jigs and fixtures and the ability to interchange such large components as boilers without individual fitting. An improved optical system was developed after the war and Cook took that to Doncaster when he became CM&EE Eastern and North Eastern Regions, and greatly increased the reliability and mileages of those regions' locomotive stocks.

When Churchward began his standardisation he was planning far into the future and had to overcome many established prejudices and outdated practices. Even in the infant motor car industry, around this period, it was extremely difficult to start from scratch. F. W. Lanchester[4] attempted this, as explained in his biography by P. W. Kingsford:[5] 'The historical importance of Lanchester's decision to go for the motor car cannot be overlooked. It ensured that development of the industry would proceed not merely from the big British companies, who were in any case at that time all working on continental patents, but also from a second source, the engineer working out his own ideas in a new, original and native design, which resulted in the first full-sized British petrol driven motor car.

'Lanchester's aim was no less than a motor car designed as such from first principles, and not an adaptation of the horse carriage. This meant designing something quite new in which there would be an absolute minimum of vibration and noise, and which could be steered safely at a speed greater than anything then on the roads. This also meant entirely new methods of manufacture.

'He had to design new machines to make many of his components, he developed a system of limits and fits, suitable for mass production and complete interchangeability of parts, and, finding in the environment of the road vehicle that the coarse Whitworth thread (below ¾″ diameter) was unable to withstand vibrations without nuts working loose, developed his 'M' thread many years before the similar BSF thread.'

There had been numerous attempts at various types of locomotive standardisation before Churchward, but these were usually either standard industrial locomotives from private builders or quantity production of selected types (eg LNWR 'DX' 0-6-0). Occasionally the same pattern of cylinders, wheels, boilers, etc were used on different classes of locomotive but no attempt had been made to introduce any real interchangeability.

Large scale production of a single type, re-vamped every decade or so reached its peak in Russia. For example, the 'S' type 2-6-2 passenger engine of 1910, designed and built at Sormovo ran to about 900; an improved version the 'Su' built at Kolomna from 1925 was built with detail modifications (Sum) until 1951 and an all-time total of 3,750 locomotives.

The Engineering Standards Committee referred to previously at the request of the Government of India undertook the standardisation of locomotives in 1903; whether Churchward was asked for his opinions is not known but it was quite likely. He was elected to the Association of Railway Locomotive Engineers on 13 June 1902, having been proposed by Wainwright and seconded by Holden. At his first meeting, S. W. Johnson was in the chair and on the agenda was a request from the Engineering Standards Committee for the ARLE to give some guidance in the matter of standardising specifications. A motion was proposed by H. A. Ivatt and seconded by T. Hurry Riches, 'That each member fill in particulars on the form which will be sent by Mr Churchward, who has kindly undertaken to tabulate the same, with a view to arriving at a Standard Specification for Materials, to be used in the construction of Locomotives, Carriages and Wagons.' It was carried unanimously.

One of Churchward's first moves in building his design team at Swindon was to have the drawing office employees transferred from a weekly wage to salaried employment. This was agreed by the Locomotive and C&W Committee of the Board on 8 October 1902. There were 37 draughtsmen on the books plus one at Wolverhampton. Top of the list was G. H. Burrows. Twenty-third on the list was O. E. F. Deverell who, within a few years was leading locomotive draughtsman and later became Assistant Chief Draughtsman to Burrows. Following Burrows' death in 1923 he became Chief-Draughtsman but tragically he too died in harness in 1925 at the early age of 50. He was most unusual in that he had served a seven-year works apprenticeship whereas most draughtsmen had been engineering apprentices and finished off in the test house. Burrows, who had had a great deal to do with Churchward's early boiler development and the design work on 4-6-0 No 100 gradually became remote from the day to day work of the drawing office and without doubt it was Deverell who was able to interpret Churchward's ideas in the drawing office, where as has been told many times, Churchward was a regular visitor.

Churchward also introduced a rationale into development testing and appointed J. W. Cross and G. H. Pearson as junior assistants in the locomotive works and their contributions were enormous. G. H. Pearson later went to the SECR as Works Manager at Ashford and assistant to Maunsell; he took Holcroft with him. Cross went into the internal combustion engine field.

The only locomotive that bore a direct resemblance to the original scheme that was built, and can be considered the experimental prototype, was No 100 which was put to traffic in February 1903. Future engines all had 10in piston valves and taper boilers, and modified cylinder and motion design. It lasted, with reboilering, over 30 years, until June 1932 when its cylinders reached the reboring limit.

Above:
Lake Shore & Michigan Southern Rail road 2-6-2 No 4670. The American type of cylinder construction, with saddle to support the drumhead smokebox, can clearly be seen. Churchward may well have built his 'big' engine as a two-cylinder 2-6-2 had he not gone for 4-cylinders before design started, and hence *The Great Bear* might have looked a little like this.
Author's collection

Right:
It has been suggested that the two-outside cylinder 2-6-0s of the MSWJ somehow influenced Churchward. One of them became GWR No 24 and was reboilered. It was known as 'Galloping Alice' and had the distinction of hauling an up Bristol express into Swindon following the failure of 'King' No 6003! (Above) As MSWJ No 16
Author's collection

Below right:
After GW modifications as No 24. *Lens of Sutton*

Above:
One of Dean's 'Badminton' class 4-4-0s, the first GWR class to appear with the Belpaire-type firebox (this being attributed to Churchward). These were very free running, strong engines, forerunners of the 'Atbaras' and 'Cities'. *Real Photos (15230)*

Right:
No 3310 *Waterford* the final 'Badminton' was turned out with the second S/2 boiler; the first (which had a dome) had been put on the 5ft 8in 'Duke' class 4-4-0 No 3312 *Bulldog*. *Real Photos (T5016)*

Below:
No 3359 *Kingsbridge* one of the 'Camel' class with the early production S/2 boiler, as earmarked for the three smaller types in his standard engine scheme. *Lens of Sutton*

Above:
No 3297 *Earl Cawdor* as fitted in July 1903 with the experimental boiler that it carried for just over three years. Inspired by F. G. Wright, Churchward's Assistant, it did not cause Churchward to deviate from his plans. *Real Photos (15231)*

Right:
'Six-wheel coupled bogie goods' No 2601, known as 'Krüger'. Another nine appeared but with pony trucks in place of the bogie – incidentally the only Dean suspension bogie with *inside frames* fitted to a locomotive. Following this class Churchward rejected traditional GW double frames, inside cylinders, inclined cylinders, and the combustion chamber, for his large locomotives. *Real Photos (T7512)*

Below right:
A rare action shot of 'Krüger' on a heavy mixed goods train. *Author's collection*

Above:
No 100, Churchward's first outside-cylinder 4-6-0 as built, in early 1902. *Real Photos (1764)*

Left:
No 100 after being named *Dean* in June 1902. *Real Photos (18246)*

Below left:
In November 1902 the name was altered to *William Dean*. *Real Photos (12201)*

Above right:
No 100 was again fitted with different nameplates in 1904 as shown here but it has also been fitted with a short-coned boiler and the tender has fenders instead of coal rails and an unusual tall thin mushroom air-vent, probably indicating the fitting of an early version of water scoop. *Real Photos (1766)*

Right:
No 100 was finally withdrawn in June 1932 as 2900 in the condition shown. It was in service for over 30 years. *Real Photos (10646)*

2
Some Technical Details

Boilers

Churchward's first main locomotive preoccupation was with the boiler. This development has been very well documented elsewhere on a number of occasions and will therefore only be dealt in outline here.

In 1906, Churchward read a paper entitled *Large Locomotive Boilers* to the I. Mech. E. He opened by stating:

'The modern locomotive question is principally a question of boiler. The great increase in the size of boilers and in the pressures carried, which has taken place during the past few years, has necessitated the reconsideration of principles of design which had been worked out and settled during many years experience with comparatively small boilers carrying low pressures. The higher temperatures incidental to the higher pressures have required the provision of much more liberal water-spaces and better provision for circulation. Locomotive engineers have now apparently settled down to the use of one of the two types of boiler for very large engines, the wide firebox extending over the frames and wheels and the long narrow box sloping up over the axles behind the main drivers'.

He went on to compare the two types:

'Much more experience has been gained with the wide box in America than in this country, and so far as the author has been able to ascertain it has been found there that the poorer coals in large quantities can be burnt with much greater facility and economy in this type than in the narrow pattern. This advantage is

offset to some extent by the fact that, when standing there is considerable waste in the wide grates as compared with the narrow, and this is, of course, serious when goods trains are kept standing about as is often the case here. This disadvantage has been found on the Great Western Railway, but no doubt careful design and fitting of ashpans will keep this waste within bounds.'

No doubt here he is referring to the 'Krügers' with their wide fireboxes and combustion chambers. These engines were replaced by the smaller 'Aberdares' with No 2 (later No 4) boilers. The same fault was found in some quarters in the 1950s on the introduction of the BR standard Class 9F 2-10-0s which burnt more coal than '28xx' on trains that the latter were quite capable of dealing with. (Loose coupled freight trains could not be increased in weight or speeded up due to braking limitations and large expensive locomotives were superfluous.)

Churchward became Assistant Manager of Swindon Locomotive Works in 1895 and, following the death of Samuel Carlton, became Manager in 1896; from September 1897 he also became Chief Assistant to William Dean, Locomotive Carriage & Wagon Superintendent. He quickly made his presence felt with the 'Badminton' class 6ft, 8½in 4-4-0s built between December 1897 and January 1899 these 20 engines (Lot 109) were provided with raised Belpaire fireboxes instead of the round topped variety, originally planned. During this period the first engine of the final batch (Lot 113) of 5ft 8in 4-4-0s, the 'Dukes', No 3312 *Bulldog* was built with the prototype Standard No 2 boiler. The last 'Badminton', No 3312 *Waterford* was turned out three months later, in January 1899 with the second No 2 boiler. This had no dome and was provided with a steel firebox, an experiment

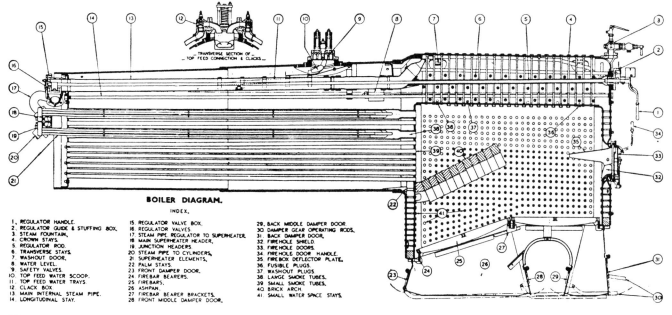

BOILER DIAGRAM.

INDEX.

1. REGULATOR HANDLE.	15. REGULATOR VALVE BOX.	29. BACK MIDDLE DAMPER DOOR.
2. REGULATOR GUIDE & STUFFING BOX.	16. REGULATOR VALVES.	30. DAMPER GEAR OPERATING RODS.
3. STEAM FOUNTAIN.	17. STEAM PIPE. REGULATOR TO SUPERHEATER.	31. BACK DAMPER DOOR.
4. CROWN STAYS.	18. MAIN SUPERHEATER HEADER.	32. FIREHOLE SHIELD.
5. REGULATOR ROD.	19. JUNCTION HEADERS.	33. FIREHOLE DOORS.
6. TRANSVERSE STAYS.	20. STEAM PIPE TO CYLINDERS.	34. FIREHOLE DOOR HANDLE.
7. WASHOUT DOOR.	21. SUPERHEATER ELEMENTS.	35. FIREBOX DEFLECTOR PLATE.
8. WATER LEVEL.	22. PALM STAYS.	36. FUSIBLE PLUGS.
9. SAFETY VALVES.	23. FRONT DAMPER DOOR.	37. WASHOUT PLUGS.
10. TOP FEED WATER SCOOP.	24. FIREBAR BEARERS.	38. LARGE SMOKE TUBES.
11. TOP FEED WATER TRAYS.	25. FIREBARS.	39. SMALL SMOKE TUBES.
12. CLACK BOX.	26. ASHPAN.	40. BRICK ARCH.
13. MAIN INTERNAL STEAM PIPE.	27. FIREBAR BEARER BRACKETS.	41. SMALL WATER SPACE STAYS.
14. LONGITUDINAL STAY.	28. FRONT MIDDLE DAMPER DOOR.	

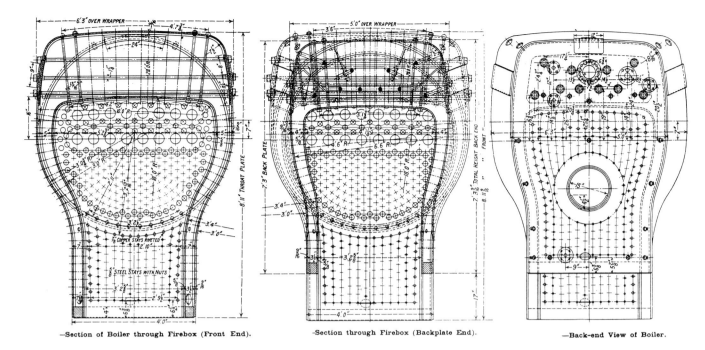

-Section of Boiler through Firebox (Front End).   -Section through Firebox (Backplate End).   -Back-end View of Boiler.

repeated at intervals throughout the Great Western's existence but without becoming orthodox practice. In October a single engine appeared to Lot 120 No 3352 *Camel*. This had the third No 2 boiler; raised Belpaire firebox, parallel domeless boiler, drum-head smokebox and cast iron chimney. This 5ft 8in 4-4-0 was the prototype for an eventual 156 engines many rebuilt from 'Dukes' including *Bulldog* after which the class was later named. All eventually received coned boilers, if not built with them. In December appeared No 2601 a 4-6-0, 'six-coupled bogie goods' nicknamed 'Krüger'. It was over two years before there were any further developments on the standard boiler front, in February of that year No 100 appeared with a similar boiler to the 'Camels' but very much larger. In September a new boiler appeared, larger than the No 2 but not as big as that of No 100. This was the prototype No 4 and was fitted to an 'Aberdare' 2-6-0, No 2661. A second standard No 4 was built and put on No 2662. This boiler however had a tapered portion reminiscent of the American 'wagon-top' boiler. It increased the steam space at the hottest part of the barrel and became a GW standard. In the same month an

'Atbara' 4-4-0, similar to the straight-framed 'Camels' but with 6ft 8½in wheels, was fitted with a coned No 4. This locomotive No 3705 *Mauritius* became the prototype 'City'. It was proposed to fit a batch of 'Bulldogs' ('Camels') with this boiler as 'Super-Bulldogs', but this never materialised. With the coming of the standard engines the boiler position was settled, apart from detail modifications. In July 1903, however, one of the 'Badmintons', No 3297 *Earl Cawdor* was rebuilt with a boiler having a distinctly North Eastern look, as also did the double side window cab. It ran for over three years with this boiler but showed no advantages over Churchward's new standards and was replaced by one of them.

The Churchward Engine

For his future standard locomotives, Churchward had a small experimental stationary steam engine built. The engine incorporated a longer valve travel and greater steam lap than

Above:
Sections through the larger S/7 boiler showing clearly the sloping shape of the firebox plates.
Railway Engineer

The standard Churchward boiler in its later form, illustrated is the S/1 as fitted to 'Saints', 'Halls' and 'Granges'.
left: **diagram showing arrangement of components**
right: **details of construction.**
GWR/Railway Engineer

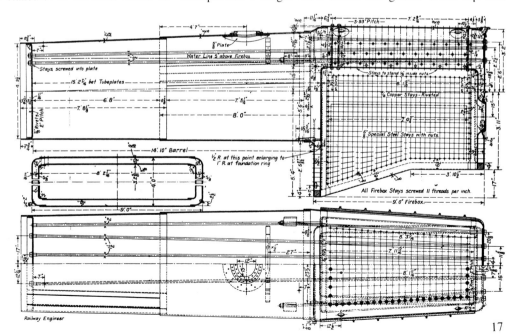

17

heretofore. The valve gear that was developed for locomotives used 10in diameter piston valves having a valve travel of 6¼in and a steam lap of 1¾in; it was first used on 4-6-0 No 98. This gear became standard on all his future 30in stroke two-cylinder engines.

Churchward himself gave some idea of the problems that he had to tackle with regard to piston valves in his contribution to the discussion on Cowan's paper on American Locomotive Practice.

'To one who had had to encounter the prejudice against piston-valves which existed all over England, it was interesting to see what a large percentage, not to say majority of the modern locomotives shown were fitted with piston-valves. From what he had gathered on the subject – and the author's observations seemed to bear it out – trouble had been experienced in America with piston valves, but American engineers meant to overcome it. On the Great Western Railway piston valves had been tried, and had given considerable trouble; they were undoubtedly one of the most troublesome pieces of mechanism with which any one could have to deal. He had set before himself the task of curing the defects, if possible; feeling quite sure that engineers would never have a chance of utilising to the utmost the power of the locomotive and bringing it, in economy, within anything like reach of the compound, without the use of piston-valves. Seeing the success attained through a long series of years with plain snap rings upon pistons 18in to 20in in diameter, running at high speeds, he did not think there was any reason to despair of getting a tight piston-valve before long. Piston-valves were supposed to use much more steam than the flat valves, and that belief was held not only widely but strongly on the Great Western Railway. Against it, however, he wished to set the experience of at least one piston-valve engine, weighing about 68ton 10cwt. [No 98 put into traffic a few weeks earlier.] This engine, on its first 4,000 miles, working the heaviest express between Bristol and Exeter, had consumed only 33.6lb of coal per mile. While piston-valves remained tight their economy was, if anything, superior to that of the ordinary flat valve.'

Many years later (1955) Sir William Stanier continued the story:[6]

'About this time, in 1906, Churchward saw particulars in the American technical press of what was called the American semi-plug piston valve. He was so impressed with the design that he purchased the rights of manufacture in this country and obtained for trial a pair of valves as made in America. The design of this valve is such that the steam rings for maintaining steam tightness are expanded by steam pressure when the regulator is open to fit the walls of the steam chest, and are locked in position by means of locking rings which are also activated by steam pressure. The fact is that when steam is shut off the rings are not in contact with the walls of the steam chest so that when drifting there is practically no wear and a very free running engine. When the regulator is open the valves maintain excellent steam-tight conditions; in practice it was found that even when there was 0.025in wear in the steam chest the valves were still steam-tight when the regulator was open. When the manufacture of these valves was first undertaken, after machining, every ring was hand-scraped so that the width over the head was not more than 0.005in around the whole periphery. This was very expensive and took time to manufacture. In the course of time, however, manufacturing processes were developed by which all of these rings could be produced on the lathe and could be assembled without any handwork being required. A valve of this kind inevitably took some time to get into proper production and the

organisation for maintaining it was built up over a number of years. It has, however, given extremely good results in service on the Great Western Railway, I refrained from introducing it when I went to the London Midland & Scottish Railway, as by that time the simple narrow rings in the piston-valve head grooves gave quite good results.'

Following Sir William's paper (to the Newcomen Society) Harold Holcroft added some further remarks on this subject in a written communication. He said:

'In my view it is to be regretted that Sir William refrained from taking the semi-plug piston valve over to the LMS for had he done so it is probable that this valve would have been adopted by British Railways. It has been suggested that the type of valve would not stand up to high superheat, but a set of heads was obtained from Swindon and tried out about 1920 on one of Maunsell's 'N' class engines on the South Eastern & Chatham Railway, which also had 10in long travel valves; so it was easy to substitute them for heads fitted with the Schmidt broad ring. The degree of superheat in normal heavy service was about 630°F in this class of engine, but I noted peaks of 700°F or more at times registered on the pyrometer when dusty coat was being fired and the box filled with luminous flame. The attraction of the semi-plug valves was their ease of manufacture, once the tooling had been set up in the machine shop, and there was little work to be done on the fitting bench. The trial valves did quite well in service but were not adopted by the SECR because the Schmidt ring at that time was giving excellent results, though it was more expensive to make, requiring a lot of work on the fitting bench. Mileages of 100,000 were quite common and some sets ran through to the third general repair with 180,000 miles to their credit, so that the valves were relatively cheap, viewed from a mileage basis.

'After grouping the Southern Railway adopted the Schmidt head as standard, but with the closing down of Ashford iron foundry and retirement of the old craftsmen, results were not the same and Eastleigh and its mechanised foundry could not produce equal results. German engineers who came over to fit an engine with the AEG pulverised coal firing heard of the trouble and recommended the valve with solid head and snap rings as developed on the German Railways. Drawings were obtained from Germany, and trials proving successful, this cheaply made piston valve was adopted as the new standard. Sir Henry Fowler became interested in it and sent members of his technical staff to investigate the position, with the result that this valve made its way on to the LMS at Derby, and was what Sir William found on his arrival there.

'From my experience of these various valve heads, I would describe the one with solid heads as "cheap and nasty". For practical reasons the head has to be a loose fit in the liner so that only the snap rings prevent live steam from passing through to exhaust. The admission, cut off and release points are nominal when related to the edge of the outer snap ring. This may not be of much consequence in running, but undue pre-admission can make starting from rest difficult at times. There is often trouble in withdrawing the solid heads at periodical examinations in sheds, due to carbonisation of rings, and I have known many cases of shed fitters struggling for days to free them. In the worst instance they were still stuck after a week's work; the men were instructed to put a hydraulic jack on the end of the valve spindle regardless of consequences. As a result the valve liners were forced out with the heads stuck fast in them. I understand that British Railways now make the back head and its liner 1/16in smaller in diameter

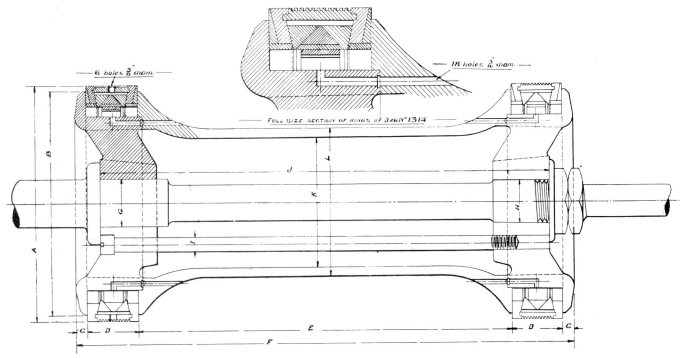

Above:
The American semi-plug piston valve as imported from the USA. This type solved Churchwards' biggest problem (ie finding a good, simple leak-free piston valve) and he bought up the British patent rights.
National Railway Museum

than the front head of the valve, for easier withdrawal, but this involves duplication of sizes in heads, liners and rings. This is a very different story to that of the piston valves introduced by Churchward and established on the Great Western Railway with such success.'

The continued use of the Stephenson (or more correctly the Howe) link motion brought a certain amount of criticism to the GWR over the years, outside Walschaerts gear being regarded as better, more modern and quite simply, the 'bees knees'. Churchward had of course used Walschaerts gear both inside, on his four-cylinder express passenger engines, and outside on the steam railmotors (and later this latter gear was used on two new and one rebuilt engines for the Vale of Rheidol Light Railway). Had he wished to change from the Stephenson type he had plenty of opportunity to do so well before his standard engines had been built in any great numbers. After World War 2 the criticism centred around 'accessibility'. All railway companies, however, had a majority of inside cylinder engines (4-4-0, 0-6-0, 0-6-0T etc) whose valve motion was far less accessible than the GW gear. Many 'modern' express locomotives of other companies, especially those with three-cylinders and three sets of motion needed a Harry Houdini to get into (and out of) the inside set. In any case with an increase in periods between maintenance and improving facilities, any problem would be likely to decrease. It can however be admitted that some reduction in lubrication points and trials with needle bearings could have been attempted by the GWR but patently weren't. The benefits of the GW system however outweighed all other considerations, certainly up to World War 2. The bulk of the gear lay between the frames in space not required for anything else, it was also rigidly held in alignment and as it

needed less attention than other parts, it did not need to be dismantled (and then reset) as did the Walschaerts. With no connections at the crosshead, pistons could be removed; with no return crank the side rods could be removed and replaced, and the large and small ends dealt with. The piston valves too could also be removed and repaired, all without needing a pit. This left accurate valve setting to be carried out using a rig at Swindon specially developed for the purpose. As all the component parts were common to almost all the standard classes (with the exception of shorter eccentric rods on the '28xx' and '38xx' and general variations in valve rod length, their production could be rationalised and in fact was performed using a series of jigs and fixtures specially designed for the job.

It has been usual to cite the USA as changing over to Walschaerts gear universally and to imply the GW should have done the same. In America however, long travel – long lap valves were unknown and when these did become a feature those builders and railroads using them went for the Baker-Pilliod gear. This was first used in the early years of the century together with other alternatives for outside application such as the Young and the Alfred-Hubbell gears. Its main purpose was to eliminate the shifting link on the Walschaerts gear which was a source of trouble especially when longer travel was required, as an excessive swing resulted in a wedging action on the die block in the link and this had a detrimental effect on the gear. The Baker gear also gave a quicker opening and closing to steam. In its early form it was assembled from a large number of parts but many of these were replaced by a single cast frame, supporting the rest of the mechanism. The total weight of the moving components was less than that for a similar Walschaerts gear. By 1943 it was claimed that in the USA 15,000 locomotives were fitted with this type. The gear was generally ignored in Britain although 'LBSC' the model engineer used it. In a letter to the *Railway Gazette* he explained:

'The Baker valve gear was introduced into the country by the undersigned about 16 years ago. Being interested in valve gears and having done much research work, I was convinced that the gear was superior to anything in use on British railways, and to

that end built a small 4-6-2 locomotive combining what I considered the best points in British and American practice, including Baker gear. This engine was shown working under compressed air at a meeting of the Institution of Locomotive Engineers, . . . and it was there examined by the late Sir H. Fowler and the late Sir H. N. Gresley, both of whom were interested but not to the extent of trying it on one of their locomotives.

'A director of the Great Western Railway Co the late Sir A. Brocklebank, recognised the merits of the gear, and brought the CME Mr C. B. Collett to my home . . . and the little locomotive was demonstrated in steam and Mr Collett remarked on the low fuel consumption. Sir A. Brocklebank suggested that a 'Saint' class 4-6-0 then in the shops, should be fitted with the Baker gear and run in competition with a standard locomotive. I offered to drive the Baker-fitted engine (I am an old LB & SCR engineman) and guaranteed to show a saving both in running and maintenance costs; but because of the sudden unexpected death of the director, the project never got any farther. Later Mr R. E. L. Maunsell, accompanied by Mr Clayton, called at my home and saw the locomotive but although I made a small model of the gear and presented in to Mr Maunsell, nothing came of it.'[7]

It is perhaps with regard to valve setting and cylinder performance that much debate has been directed. Harry Holcroft who had a great deal of experience with both Stephenson link motion of the GW type, and Walschaerts gear (with long travel piston valves) as used on the SECR, and later the SR, by Maunsell, wrote to the *Engineer* in 1947.[8]

'My experience of engines so fitted [ie with Stephenson link motion] is that they are much livelier in acceleration and running than similar engines fitted with Walschaerts gear. For a given cut-off in the region of 25% there is a greater opening at admission and exhaust, with the consequence that the mep and ihp

are increased for a given cylinder diameter and boiler pressure. This is made clear by the valve diagrams, A representing a gear with variable lead increasing to 5/16in at 25% cut-off, while B is that for a gear with a constant lead of 3/16in. It will be appreciated that A gives 33% more area in the opening to steam and 19° more angular movement of the crankshaft during which the exhaust valve is full open.'

He went on to advocate a locomotive fitted with outside Stephenson link motion and about a year later in fact an LMS Class 5 No 4767 was built at Crewe with just such a gear, under the authority of H. G. Ivatt. This locomotive, now happily preserved and in working order, was remembered by Campbell Highet when shedmaster at Bank Hall:

'One of the Black Fives built in 1947. This engine had outside Stephenson valve gear; she was the only one of her kind. We had her at Bank Hall for a time, and a very strong engine she was, indeed some said she was the strongest Class 5 ever.'

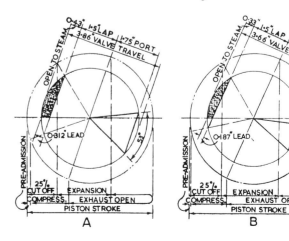

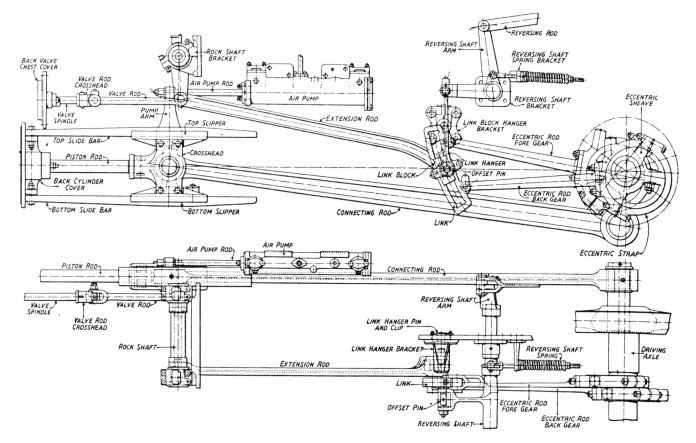

A characteristic of the Stephenson link motion is that the lead varies with the cut-off. This is the pre-admission to steam just before the end of the stroke and is usually ⅛in to ³⁄₁₆in and stays constant in the Walschaerts gear. Churchwards' early experiments however convinced him to adjust the gear so as to give a negative lead at starting and in full gear. This eliminated any compression at starting and enhanced starting acceleration and hill-climbing ability. At least one American railroad introduced extra linkages into Walschaerts gear in order to produce variable lead; the Denver, Rio Grande & Western Railroad did so with their Class M-68 4-8-4s by fitting a combination lever of variable proportions, ostensibly to aid the starting of heavy loads.

At higher speeds and short cut-offs there is a certain amount of compression this has a cushioning effect and does not constitute much negative work as the piston velocity has almost reached zero (at dead centre), indeed the compression prevents the clearance volume being filled with fresh steam at the same time as heating the steam in the ports between the piston and cylinder cover, thus lessening initial condensation. On the Great Western the clearance volume was kept very low and helped to reduce cylinder losses and the need for higher superheat.

The Swindon Superheater

The superheater as developed by Churchward has received some criticism over the years due to its giving a lower maximum temperature; however it was a very effective piece of equipment as far as the GWR was concerned, for many, many years. When it was found necessary to increase the output of certain locomotive types due to very much altered service conditions following World War 2, Swindon drawing office had no difficulty in finding the correct solution.

Churchward first installed a superheater on a new '29xx' class locomotive, No 2901 *Lady Superior*. This was built with the Schmidt equipment in May 1906 and was the first modern superheater engine to run in Britain. It had the working pressure reduced from 225 to 200lb/sq.in and the cylinder diameter increased from 18in to 18⅜in; this resulted in a reduction in tractive effort from 23,090lb to 21,457lb (at 85% boiler pressure).

Between 1906 and 1909 there were a number of variant superheaters installed for testing and surveillance and in June 1909 it was decided to standardise on the Swindon No 3 pattern.

In his report to the GWR Board dated 29 June 1906 Churchward first raised the subject of superheating:

'Since my last report, one of the 4-6-0 type has been fitted with a superheater and, although it has been running too short a time to pronounce definitely upon the results, the economy shown up to the present is remarkable and is far beyond any results which have anywhere been obtained by the compound principle. There are drawbacks in the way of extra costs and probably troubles with the burning out of the superheater pipes, as well as the difficulty of keeping valves, glands etc. tight with the very high temperature of steam, but even in the face of these drawbacks the results are such that we must certainly pursue the experiment at once.'

On 13 December 1909, he wrote:

'The superheaters continue to give good results and it is found that the consumption of coal is reduced by about 12%, and the consumption of water by 20%. In addition to this, the power of the engine is increased, and this is of great importance on such trains as the Plymouth "Limited" and the Fishguard "Ocean Specials", on which the full power of the present locomotive is required. The actual saving of coal is, of course, greater on the 2-8-0 mineral engines as the coal burnt per mile is much greater than that on any of the passenger services. We are therefore giving the mineral engines the preference at present in fitting the new superheaters.'

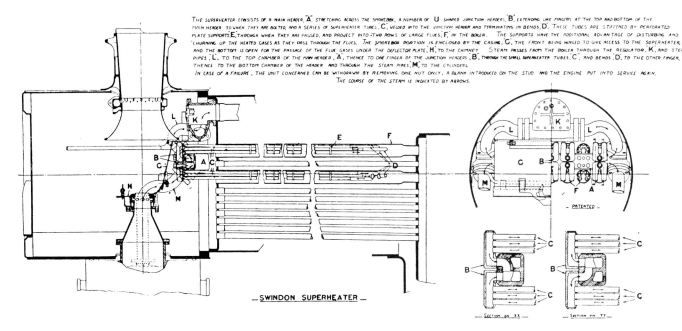

The superheater consists of a main header, A, stretching across the smokebox, a number of U shaped junction headers, B, extending like fingers at the top and bottom of the main header to which they are bolted and a series of superheater tubes, C, welded into the junction header and terminating in bends, D. These tubes are stiffened by perforated plate supports, E, through which they are passed, and project into two rows of large flues, F, in the boiler. The supports have the additional advantage of disturbing and churning up the heated gases as they pass through the flues. The smokebox portion is enclosed by the casing, G, the front being hinged to give access to the superheater and the bottom is open for the passage of the flue gases under the deflector plate, H, to the chimney. Steam passes from the boiler through the regulator, K, and steam pipes, L, to the top chamber of the main header, A, thence to one finger of the junction headers, B, through the small superheater tubes, C, and bends, D, to the other finger, thence to the bottom chamber of the header and through the steam pipes, M, to the cylinders.
In case of a failure, the unit concerned can be withdrawn by removing one nut only, a blank introduced on the stud and the engine put into service again. The course of the steam is indicated by arrows.

_ SWINDON SUPERHEATER _

_ PATENTED _

_ Section on XX _   _ Section on YY _

On 31 December 1910 he returned to the subject:

'. . . on figures taken over a period of six months, those in service have shown an average over-all economy of 12½% in fuel and 20-25% in water. The economy is not so great with the more modern and efficient engines as with some of the older types.

'In some of the latter the fuel runs to 16%. Incidentally, a great advantage is found in the employment of superheaters by reason of the engines being able to go much longer distances without taking water. The very heavy wear and tear of the boilers and fireboxes is also moderated to some extent in the engines fitted with superheaters'.

In 1914 Henry Fowler (later Sir Henry) of the Midland Railway read a now famous paper to the Institution of Civil Engineers entitled *Superheating Steam in Locomotives*. Many senior locomotive engineers contributed to the discussion or sent written communications, both from Britain and abroad. Churchward made some very characteristic remarks:
'. . . he would say, to paraphrase an Americanism, "it is the coal-pile that talks". The Great Western had been fitting superheaters for some years, but they had not done much in the way of making experiments . . . If engineers waited until innumerable experiments had been made to define the last degree of superheat that could be obtained, they might miss a good deal of coal in the interval.'

It is not proposed to put the case for and against high superheat in any great detail but suffice to say that theoretical considerations are very different from railway operating ones. A major problem, that of lubrication and the carbonisation of piston valves was never completely solved, and the cost of increased maintenance here could wipe out any gains through coal saving. The very last European express passenger locomotives, the two Class 10 4-6-2s built for the Deutsches Bundesbahn by Krupp in 1957 had a control that sprayed water into the superheater header should the temperature reach 450°C. Although Churchward had teased a little with regard to experimenters, he certainly made sure that he had a perfectly adequate lubricator for his superheater. He tested a number of mechanical lubricators and one engine, No 177

Robertson was fitted with both a mechanical type and a GW sight-feed hydrostatic type and tested using each alternatively every other month. The latter was adopted and a special feature was a link with the regulator that fed oil to the valves and cylinders while running with the regulator shut. Production of superheater units was gradually streamlined until in 1930s there was a jig and fixture production line. Churchward prepared a report to the International Railway Congress in July 1914 but due to the war he could not present it until 1921; he included statistics for the number of superheater locomotives in service and revised them where he was able for 1921.[10]

The exhaust steam injector

The exhaust steam injector was manufactured under licence at Swindon and fitted to all Churchward's larger engines. It was gradually modified over the years but was found to be a reliable and cheap feed water heater and suited the GWR although other companies, possibly due to poor water, didn't have the same success. Test results of 7916 *Mobberley Hall* are reproduced in tabular form (see chapter 7) and show how extremely useful this piece of equipment was. These figures also illustrate vividly the margin between two distinctly different types of coal.

Jumper top variable blast pipe

This was very effective up to World War 2 as an automatic but very simple device. It did not find favour on the LMS or LNER where it was tried, but interestingly the recently preserved Vulcan Foundry 4-8-4 presented to the National Railway Museum in York by the Chinese People's Republic is still fitted with the apparatus, so one must assume that when designed and proportioned properly it worked well.

Top feed

This distinctive Great Western feature was introduced in 1911. With this arrangement feed water was fed onto perforated trays in

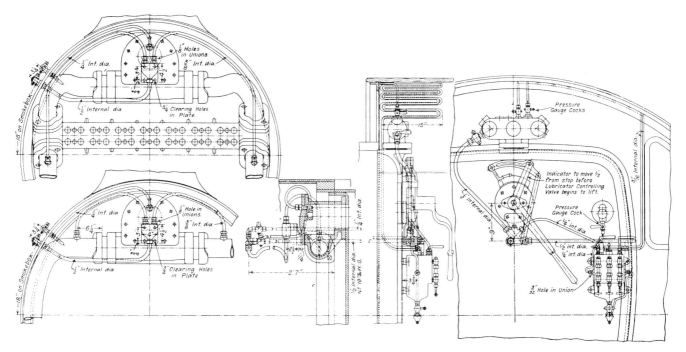

Above left:
The Churchward superheater as standardised with the regulator in the smokebox *GWR*

Above:
The sight-feed lubricator arrangement for the regulator and cylinders
Railway Engineer

Below:
The jumper-top blast pipe. When suitably matched and sized for any particular design, this was the most effective variable blast-pipe ever designed. *Railway Engineer*

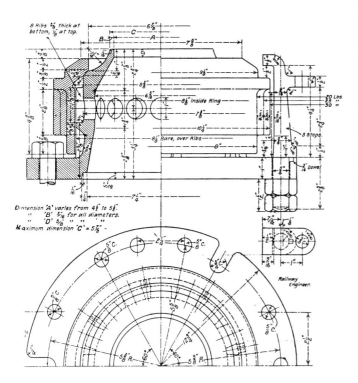

the steam space and finally mixed in with the boiler water at a temperature only 40°F below the latter. The biggest proportion of any solid matter in the feed water was deposited on the trays which could easily be removed for cleaning. Any further solids were dispersed as sludge and easily removed at washouts whereas before top feed they had built up in certain areas and caused severe corrosion of boiler plates. Churchward of course introduced water softening plants at a number of locations and increased the locations of water-troughs. Neither the GW top feed clacks or the use of a domeless boiler 'travelled' well, especially on to the LMS whose system could show a complete variation in quality of water supply and often serious foaming and almost inevitable priming occurred. (Due often also perhaps to crews keeping their water levels *far* too high.) Churchward only used those fittings and accessories that could be quickly standardised into reliable components. He shunned the idea of fitting out his engines with all the trappings and accoutrements in the railway industry's catalogue. In fact the rift between Swindon and the then infant Institution of Locomotive Engineers came about because of this as recounted by Holcroft:[11]

'In order to attempt to interest the Great Western in the Institution an invitation was issued to Swindon to send a small party to hear the reading of a paper and enter into the discussion upon it. At that period Swindon Works was like a fortress which no one could enter without credentials and no information as to what was going on inside was issued to the press or public except through official channels. The invitation was accepted with an exploratory end in view, to ascertain at first-hand whether the new Institution was one which should receive their active support. A few men were selected having experience in the subject under discussion and they were briefed beforehand as to the limits to what they could or should not say. The presence of visitors from Swindon at the meeting was too good an opportunity to miss for some of those present, not necessarily members, to buttonhole them and try to interest the visitors in the specialities of the firms to which they belonged, while others endeavoured to find out more as to what was going on inside the works. After this badgering was experienced on a second occasion an unfavourable impression was created and Swindon withdrew into its "splendid isolation". The Great Western alone among the larger railways was not

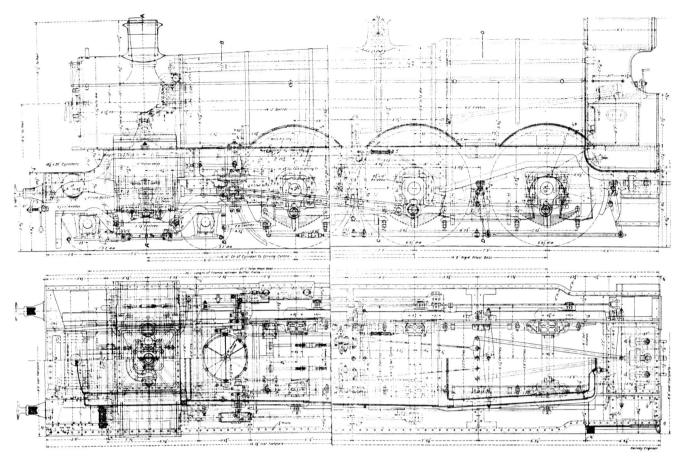

represented by members in the Institution for the next 20 years or more.'

Most attempts to improve on Churchward's work in Britain have been directed at the engine cycle thermal efficiency. The misguided nature of this was due rather to a misinterpretation over many years of Sadi Carnot. Professor Ivo Kolin pointed out:[12]

'Carnot generalises his observations regardless of any actual engine or working mechanism – his description of the cycle contains no engineering details. Carnot's engine would not be economical due to numerous engineering problems, which are technically much more important than the advantage of the ideal cycle. The ideal cycle is one thing: its practical realisation is another. The final criterion of economy of an engine is not thermodynamic efficiency, but specific fuel consumption. The best thermodynamic cycle is, by itself, no assurance of low fuel consumption. On the contrary, the opposite case is quite possible if significant conditions are forgotten. Here is the source of all misinterpretations of Carnot's ideas. Carnot himself was not solely concerned with the object of achieving the best possible efficiency. On the contrary, at the end of his book he says: ''The attempts made to approach this result would be even more harmful than useful, if other important considerations were neglected''.

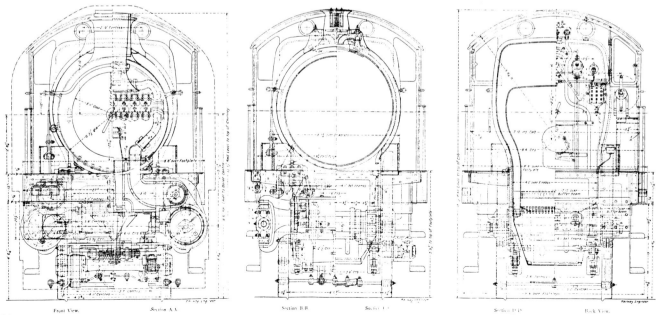

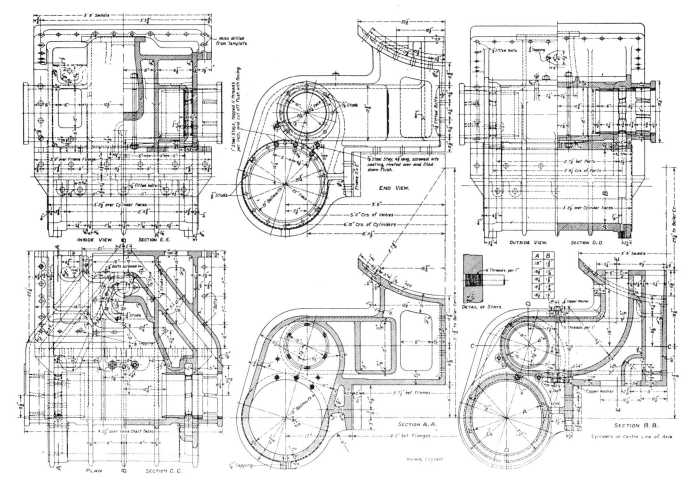

The continual repetition and theoretical description of the cycle had the result that all attention had been wrongly directed in futile attempts to realise it.'

Carnot in fact, who wrote his *Réflexions sur la puissance motrice du feu* as long ago as 1824, and who died in 1832 at the age of 34, had already noticed a certain amount of engineering degeneracy with engines of his own age.

'The engines which were originally well conceived were spoiled in the hands of unskilled constructors, who, wanting to introduce improvements of lesser importance, neglected essential considerations which they would not appreciate.'

Carnot's final sentence sums up Churchward's abilities:

'To be able to evaluate, in any case, by their real value the representatable considerations of usefulness and economy, to be able to distinguish more important ones from those which are only accessory, to balance them all mutually in a convenient way, in order to achieve the best results by the easiest means, such should be the talent of the man invited to manage, co-ordinate among similar works, and to make them compete in order to reach a useful aim of any kind.'

Above left:
The general arrangement for the final batches of Churchward two-cylinder 4-6-0s – the 'Courts'. The bar extension to the frames at the front end can be see. *Railway Engineer*

Left:
Cross sections through the 'Courts'. The enormous steam chest volume on the inlet side can be clearly seen, a major reason for the success of the Churchward engines. Later cylinders with outside steam pipes did not perform so well (although better than their LMS and BR counterparts); the 'Granges' however had much enlarged steam chests. *Railway Engineer*

Above:
Churchward's standard pattern of 30in stroke cylinder, wherein lay the reasons for much of his locomotives' success. The later outside steampipe pattern was not quite as good until the 'Granges' whose cylinder design was superb. *Railway Engineer*

Right:
The later Churchward cab layout, with screw reverse. No frills, no unnecessary duplication and nothing to cause confusion in the event of a footplate emergency. *Railway Engineer*

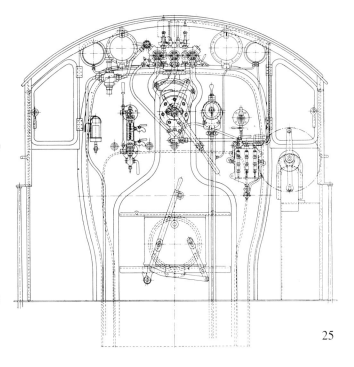

3
The Standard Two-Cylinder Engines

The appearance of 4-6-0 No 98 in March 1903 was one of the major turning points in British locomotive history, it was the forerunner of hundreds of locomotives in this country. It was not the first British 4-6-0 with outside cylinders built for express passenger services and as its main improved features were not easily visible, the reasons for its success did not become common practice on the rest of Britains' railways for a quarter of a century. Except that is, for some engines built at Ashford from 1917, but here the gospel had been taken directly by two of Churchward's apostles from Swindon.

Of the six types which appeared in Churchward's original scheme it was only the 5ft 8in 4-6-0 that didn't appear in his lifetime. In addition, one 4-6-0 (No 171 *Albion*) was rebuilt as a 4-4-2 to run against *La France* , the imported de Glehn compound and this resulted in 13 express engines being built as 4-4-2s, although they were all converted to 4-6-0s later. There were developments of the 2-6-2Ts in the form of the 2-8-0T and the 2-6-0; the later type itself being enlarged into a 5ft 8in 2-8-0. A smaller series was also partly developed with the same Churchward features but of much smaller dimensions and with 17in × 24in cylinders. A planned 0-8-0PT of this type was not forthcoming, neither was a series of inside framed, inside cylinder engines with piston valves, to replace old double framed engines. At the bottom end of the scale the successful railmotors were developed. 0-6-0 locomotives whether tank or tank types seem to have been anathema to Churchward and his usual rule was to scrap them, although, as many were relatively new, Belpaire boilers were fitted at boiler renewal and saddle tanks were replaced by the introduction of the pannier type on a large scale. His successors, Collett and Hawksworth were to build vast quantities of these as new construction.

The following are notes on some of the standard classes, quotations enclose remarks from Churchwards reports to his directors and dates of the reports are in brackets.

'County' class 6ft 8½in. 4-4-0

'[Ref 1][13] is an engine slightly lighter than the "City" class, 10 of which have been constructed with a view to provide greater power over sections of the line, such as Oxford to the North and Bristol to Shrewsbury, upon which the trains are becoming very heavy, and the bridges are not capable of carrying the heavier engines. They can also be used for fast Goods trains when necessary instead of older patterns of the same class, but with inside cylinders which are at present employed. (12-12-1904).

'The "County" class 4-4-0, have been working very satisfactorily indeed. For their weight 55ton 6cwt they are quite the most powerful engine we have ever seen. One of them on trial with 10 eight-wheeled carriages, stopped dead in the middle of Hemerdon incline and started the train again taking it over the top

of the bank without assistance. On account of this great power, there is vibration at high speed, which is some little discomfort to the drivers, but this is just the same sort of thing that is found in steamships of very high power. The engines, however, run with perfect steadiness on the road, and pass through the junctions and fittings at stations very smoothly. (15-7-1905.)

'These engines have continued to do good work. The class was specially designed with the view of getting great hauling power with the lightest possible weight for use with fast trains on some of our lighter working. On this account more vibration than usual was experienced on the footplate tending to prejudice the use of the engine for high speed trains. We have now, I think, devised means which will eliminate this vibration and, if this is successfully accomplished, we should certainly have a further number of the class, for they are much cheaper and lighter than the 4-6-0 or 4-4-2 classes and quite powerful enough for a large portion of our trains. (5-12-1905.)

'After some experience, we have succeeded in arriving at a method of balancing this type which has effected a very considerable improvement in the running and with much more comfort to the men. I trust it will also have the effect of reducing wear and tear to some extent.' (4-8-1908.)

'Saint' class 6ft 8½in 4-6-0

'[Ref 2 and 2a] illustrate the heaviest and most powerful type of passenger engine we have built, two being in service and six more under construction. The engine shown in [Ref 2] with 200 lb/sq in pressure ran the "Limited" train from Plymouth during July, August and September, and performed the service well. Some of these have 200 lb/sq in pressure and the remainder 225 lb/sq in as shown in [Ref 2a]. (12-12-1904.)

'The class are doing very satisfactory work and are employed in hauling the Plymouth Limited Expresses. On the 24th ultimo, one of these engines – *Robins Bolitho*, took 15 eight-wheeled coaches on the 10.50 am Paddington to Bristol. She arrived five minutes late; six minutes were however, due to traffic delay so that one minute was made up in running. (15-7-1905)

'With regard to the work done by the various types of engine the tendency is to employ the 4-4-0 and 4-6-0 passenger engines for the hauling of goods trains instead of the old standard goods engines which have previously been utilised for this purpose. At the present time, we have about 45 passenger engines working daily on goods trains. These engines are of course, more expensive machines than the old engines for the purpose, but great advantage is found by the Traffic Department in so far as the speed and timekeeping of the trains is much improved and congestion of the line is avoided.' (13-12-1909.)

'28xx' class 4ft 7½in 2-8-0

'The heaviest class of Goods tender engine we have built, one is in service and 20 more are under construction. The engine shown is at present running 60 wagon coal trains between Severn tunnel Junction and Paddington and doing the work well; the weight of this train behind the tender is 920 tons.

'The load from Severn Tunnel Junction to Stoke Gifford is 45 wagons and two brake vans (with assistance through the Tunnel) as against 35 wagons and two vans, the load for the older goods engines (also with assistance through the Tunnel) and from Stoke Gifford to Paddington 60 wagons and one van =920 tons. The engine would certainly take a heavier load on the Stoke Gifford and Paddington section, but 60 wagons are all that can be conveniently dealt with at the present moment. It should be observed that the boiler, cylinders, valves and valve motion, axles, axle bosses connecting rods etc., are of the same standard as those on the large express engines of the "Albion" ["Saint"] class, the extra power being obtained by reducing the diameter of the wheels and coupling eight of them together. (12-12-1904.)

'These are doing very well and are, I think, the best type for our heavy coal trains for roads where they can be permitted. (5-12-1905.)

'There is a limit to the number of trains of great weight for which this class of engine is required, so that probably for some little time the further ten of the class which we have under construction will prove sufficient.' (29-6-1906.)

'County Tank' 6ft 8½in 4-4-2

'[Ref 5] The sample engine of this class has now been running experimentally and is found to be one of the steadiest at high speed with which we have had experience. The weight is great – about 75 ton – but, as there is no tender, the engine should prove very economical for passenger trains within the capacity of the boiler, which is, of course, less than that of the large tender engines. The engine may be run either end forward which is a great convenience, especially when the crowded condition of, say Paddington is considered. (5-12-1905.)

'This class continues to do good work and is suitable for either passenger or goods trains. The other nine engines of the class are well in hand and I trust to have them at work this autumn.' (29-6-1906.)

'31xx' class 5ft 8in 2-6-2T.

'[Ref 6] is a similar engine [to Ref 5] arranged for goods trains, having six wheels coupled instead of four. One of these engines is in service and doing very good work on heavy coal trains. 20 are under construction for the purpose of working the coal trains over the Monmouthshire Valley section. If successful, the result will be a saving of a large number of the present smaller engines. (12-12-1904.)

'21 engines are now in service, and have quite fulfilled our expectations in taking very heavy mineral trains in the Monmouthshire District. They are also suitable for passenger trains not running long distances. Upon a special trial being made of one some time since, the engine attained a speed of 75mph and ran with complete steadiness. (15-7-1905.)

'These engines are continuing to give excellent results and have effected considerable saving in the working of heavy coal and goods trains. One of these is hauling a 70 wagon train between Banbury and Southall and is doing the round trip in the day with one set of men. (5-12-1905.)

'This is one of the most useful types we have. Since my last report their use has been extended and, in the case of the Cockett bank, the improvement effected in the working of the trains and the loads hauled has been very marked.' (29-6-1906.)

Forty of these locomotives were built, the very last locomotive of the final batch being used as a prototype for another class by the fitting of the larger Standard No 4 boiler. This engine begat a further 40 of these, the '3150' class No 3150 itself, built in April 1906 may have inspired the building of a 'County Tank', No 2230 with an S/4 boiler in October, but this was very short lived due to excess weight and was rebuilt with an S/2 in January 1907, to conform with the rest of the class.

The success of the '3150' class resulted in the production of another ten-wheeled tank engine with the S/4 boiler but this was of the 2-8-0T type as against the 2-6-2T, and fitted with 4ft

Below:
The Keystone of the Arch. Churchward's second 4-6-0, No 98, as built. This was the basis for all future GWR design and influenced design on the LMSR, SR, LNER and BR. This engine, it may be added, was lighter than the later 'light' 4-6-0s – the 'Manors'! *Real Photos (51502)*

7½in wheels, the standard for freight engines. The prototype, No 4201 was built.

'42xx' class 4ft 7½in 2-8-0T

'With a view to improving the working of the heavy mineral trains in the South Wales district engine [Ref 7] has been designed and the sample engine has just been constructed. I hope that in addition to improving the working of the mineral trains, the engine will enable the work to be done more economically than by the present 2-6-2T engines which are performing the service. If this expectation is confirmed, the construction of a number of these engines will enable the 2-6-2T class to be taken from the present services in South Wales and utilised to improve the working between Newton Abbot and Penzance and other parts of the railway. (31-12-1910.)

'The sample engine of this class has been at work in the South Wales Mineral District and is giving every satisfaction; the construction of 20 of the same class is now in hand. (18-7-1911.)

'This engine continues to give entire satisfaction, and I think a considerable number of them should be built in the future for mineral service in South Wales and elsewhere. (2-1-1912.)

'During the last half-year, 10 of this type have been built and appropriated, for working the coal traffic in the neighbourhood of Llanelly and Swansea, where the mineral traffic is very congested. The result has been that the engines are found capable of taking double the load of the ordinary 0-6-0T type previously employed here and the 10 which have been allocated to the division have replaced 20 engines of the old type and have released a corresponding number of sets of enginemen and firemen, who have been utilised to fill vacancies in other parts of the railway.' (11-7-1912.)

Above:
The other side of No 98. A front steam heating swan-neck connection has been added since the previous photograph (it was later removed). *Real Photos (17850)*

Right:
No 98 after renumbering 2998 (December 1912) and naming *Ernest Cunard* **(December 1907) and fitted with a full coned boiler, superheater, top feed and different balance weights. The bogie brakes have been removed. It never received the later type cylinders with outside steam pipes.** *Real Photos (W871)*

Below right:
One of the 1905 batch of 4-6-0s, later named *Viscount Churchill* **(1907).** *Sir Ernest Palmer* **(1924) and finally** *Lord Palmer* **(1933); it was withdrawn in November 1944. Churchward's 5ft 8in 4-6-0 planned at this time would have looked like this in every way but for the driving wheel diameter.** *Real Photos (1773)*

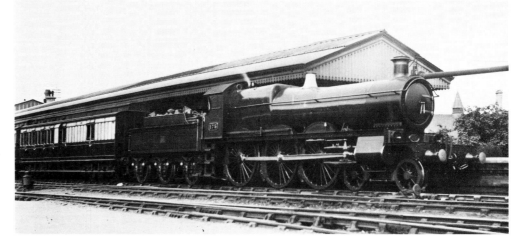

No 182 built in 1905 as a 4-4-2 one of 13, identical with the 4-6-0s and later converted, this particular locomotive in November 1912. *Real Photos (51499)*

Below:

It has been said that criticism of the angularity of Churchward's early engines produced this experimental curved fall plate and dummy front end plate frames. This was applied on to 'Atlantic' No 187 *Robertson:* **shown here after re-naming** *Bride of Lammermoor.* **It was however a heavy weight, associated with an experiment in bogie side control.** *Real Photos (2767)*

29

Left:
The prototype 'County' 4-4-0 No 3473 *County of Middlesex* as built in May 1904. Although notorious for rough riding at high speed they were also renowned for incredible bursts of hill-climbing power – especially on the Weymouth line. *Real Photos (2604)*

Below left:
One of the later 4-6-0s No 2929 *Saint Stephen* with curved ends to the footplate at the front and under the cab. Also fitted with screw reverse. *Real Photos (5061)*

Below:
The prototype Churchward 2-8-0 No 97, as built and running with a Dean 4,000 gallon tender. *British Railways*

Above right:
The second 2-8-0 No 2801 with a higher pitched boiler. Even before World War 1 these locomotives had hauled the heaviest freight trains ever (with steam locomotives) on record in Britain. *Real Photos (57204)*

Right:
Churchward's prototype 2-6-2T No 99 was introduced in 1903. Another 20 appeared in 1905, this locomotive No 3113, shown here in original condition, being the third of the batch. *Real Photos (2649)*

Below right:
The last of Lot 159 of the '31xx' 2-6-2T of 1906 was turned out with a large boiler; this became the prototype '3150' class. Shown here No 3190 was the last of the class built in January 1908. *Real Photos (2650)*

Above left:
From the '3150' class was developed a large boilered 2-8-0T with 4ft 7½in driving wheels for South Wales coal traffic. No 5203 of February 1923 is shown in the 1930s with the 'shirt button' monogram. *Real Photos (9576)*

Left:
Construction continued under Collett, with minor modifications, as the '5205' class. Latter pattern cylinders with outside steam pipes fitted. No 5225 is shown here in full passenger livery at the Railway Centenary celebrations at Darlington in 1925. *Real Photos (R3705)*

Below:
The tank engine version of the 'County' 4-4-0 was introduced in September 1905, the '2221' class known as 'County Tanks'. They carried a smaller boiler than their tender counterparts (except for one engine, but briefly). *Real Photos (51571)*

4
Mixed Traffic Engines

The most notable development from Churchward's standard engines was the building of a batch of '3150' class 2-6-2T as 2-6-0 tender engines numbered 4301–20 (no prototype was deemed necessary). He informed his Directors on 31 December 1910:

'I am of the opinion that the working of a number of the ordinary main line goods trains as distinct from mineral trains and the above mentioned fast goods trains can be considerably improved in the same manner by the provision of an engine more powerful than the old type of 0-6-0 goods engine. With this object in view, an engine has been designed and 20 of them are now under construction. I hope another useful purpose will be served by the same engines on special occasions in the hauling of heavy excursion trains. None of the parts of the engine are of new design, but are simply those employed in the construction of the 2-6-2T engine with which they are interchangeable in all respects.'

Just over a year later he told them:

'. . . our anticipations have been realised and the engine has proved so generally serviceable that I consider we should do well to replace a large number of the old 0-6-0 goods engines by 2-6-0 engines of this type. The engines are powerful enough to do very heavy goods work and at the same time have proved themselves fast and steady enough to work heavy excursion or

similar passenger trains. The practicability of using a type of engine for general purposes in this way is of very great convenience, as it obviates the necessity of keeping so varied a stock of engines in the running sheds.'

From No 4321 onwards the frames were increased in length by 9 in as it was found that the injectors and associated pipework were rather cramped. The class was in continuous production from 1913 (No 4321 onward) to 1923 and more were built in 1925 and finally a modified batch with side window cabs, in 1932. It was found, especially in severely curved areas such as Cornwall that there was a disproportinate amount of flange wear on the leading coupled wheels. To overcome this the bufferbeam was moved forward by 1ft and a heavy casting fitted behind it enabling the pony truck to perform its centring task more efficiently. The weight was increased by two tons but redistribution to the front of the engine caused the axle weight to restrict these engines to 'Red' routes. 65 engines were

Below:
The Churchward 5ft 8in 4-6-0 diagram, drawn up in 1905 but not proceeded with probably due to route availability problems. The routes they were intended for – eg the Cornish main line – could only use 'Dukes' for some years and large turntables were also not available.
National Railway Museum

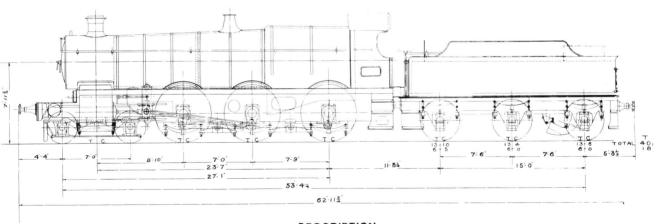

— DESCRIPTION —

CYLINDERS	DIAR 18in STROKE 30in STEAM PORTS 3½ X 1¾in EXHAUST 3½ X 4¼in
BOILER	BARREL 14-10ft ins DIAR OUTS 4-10¾ft ins & 5-6ft ins
FIREBOX	OUTS 9-0ft ins X 4-0ft ins INS 8-2¾ft ins X 3-2¼ft ins HEIGHT 6-6¾ft ins & 5-0⅞ft ins
TUBES	No 250 DIAR 2in LENGTH 15-2¼ft ins
HEATING SURFACE	TUBES 1988-65 SQ FT FIREBOX 154-26 SQ FT TOTAL 2142-91 SQ FT
AREA OF FIREGRATE	27-07 SQ FT
WHEELS	BOGIE 3-2ft ins LEADING 5-8ft ins DRIVING 5-8ft ins TRAILING 5-8ft ins
WATER CAPACITY OF TENDER	3500 GALLONS
WORKING PRESSURE	225 LBS
TRACTIVE EFFORT	28945 LBS

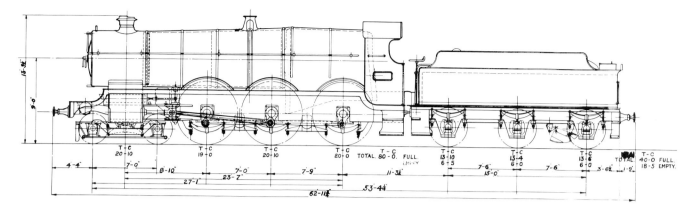

DESCRIPTION

CYLINDERS. ____ DIAR 18¼″ STROKE 30″ STEAM PORTS3¾″× 1¾″ EXHAUST 3½″× 4½″.

BOILER. ____ BARREL 14_10″ DIAR OUTS 6_0″ & 5_6″.

FIREBOX. ____ OUTS 10_0″× 4'-3″ INS 9_2⅝″× 3_2⅝″ HEIGHT 6_10⅞″ & 5_2⅞″.

TUBES. ____ {
SUPERHEATER TUBES №80. DIAR ⅝″. №24. DIAR I″. LENGTH 15_8½″.
FIRE   ″   ″ 220. ″ 2″. ″ 14. ″ 5⅝″. ″ 15_2⅞″.
}

HEATING SURFACE ____ {
SUPERHEATER TUBES 319·37 SQ FT
FIRE   ″ 2036·85 ″ ″   } TOTAL 2525·50 SQ.FT.
FIREBOX   168·28 ″ ″
}

AREA OF FIREGRATE. ____ 30·28 SQ·FT

WHEELS. ____ BOGIE 3_2″. LEADING 6_8¼″. DRIVING 6_8¼″. TRAILING 6_8¼″.

WATER CAPACITY OF TENDER. ____ 3500 GALLONS.

WORKING PRESSURE. ____ 225 LBS.

TRACTIVE EFFORT. ____ 24395 LBS.   _CLASS 4·6·0_

—— SCALE ⅛ = 1 FOOT ——

thus modified in the '53xx' series and were renumbered in the '83xx' series. Later those still in service were reconverted and renumbered.

Churchward had had drawn up a 5ft 8in 4-6-0 in 1905. This stood in relationship to the 'Saint' class 6ft 8½in 4-6-0s as did Dean's 'Duke' class 5ft 8in 4-4-0 to the 'Badminton' class 6ft 8½in 4-4-0s, the 'Dukes' being used on the hilly main lines of the far west. According to K. J. Cook, the locomotive inspectors began to ask for a 4-6-0 to replace the '43xx' engines on certain duties, as inevitably their very success caused them to be used on almost any train that came along. Churchward turned a deaf ear and turned his attention to enlarging the 2-6-0 into a 2-8-0, utilising the Standard No 1 boiler at first. C. B. Collett, as Churchward's Assistant wrote a report to the Directors dated 2 December 1919;

'The sample 2-8-0 engine, 5ft 8in wheels – No 4700 – which was turned out new from the Works on the 29 April has been quite successful for the purpose for which it was designed, viz: running of fast heavy long distance Goods traffic. The engine is stationed at Bristol, is working mainly between that station and Plymouth, and has up to the present done 25,000 miles. In regard to economy and power the design is quite satisfactory and if and when the running of fast long distance Goods train is resumed, will be very useful.'

A year later (30 November 1920) Churchward informed them;'Eight engines similar to No 4700 (2-8-0) but with larger boiler are in course of manufacture at Swindon, and it is hoped to have these ready for the summer traffic next year.'

The same statement was made the following year and it wasn't until April 1923 that the last engine of this small class (4708) was completed. The first engine had been rebuilt with the prototype Standard No 7 boiler in May 1921 and the rest of the

Above:

Churchward had plans to fit a new generation of main line engines with a larger boiler than the S/1. This boiler, the Standard No 7, was only fitted to the remainder of the '47xx' class, and later put on the prototype. The diagram for the 'Super-Saint' with this boiler; an impressive looking machine. The larger boiler would not have fitted the 6ft 8½in engines without considerable changes to the other standard parts but a 4-6-0 with the 5ft 8in wheels and this boiler would have been a formidable proposition indeed. *National Railway Museum*

class appeared with them. An enlarged series of standard engines was to be built with this boiler. Apart from the '47xx' class Churchward planned a large boilered 'Saint' and 'Star' (4 cyl.) 4-6-0s and '28xx'' 2-8-0. A number of problems appear to have ended this scheme although it is surprising that it wasn't continued in later years. The 6ft 8½in 4-6-0s would, it seems have been slightly out of gauge, although there is reason to think that the GW had definite plans to enlarge the loading gauge; this is why the 'King' class 4-6-0, when it appeared, with its much lengthened Standard No 7 boiler (the No 12) was of necessity mounted on smaller driving wheels. The idea that Collett decided on 6ft 6in wheels because he was overtaken by a '43xx' 2-6-0 whilst journeying from Swindon to Paddington is therefore a little ridiculous. That it decided him on a 6ft 0in two-cylinder 4-6-0 however, is a different 'kettle of fish' and may well have triggered the rebuilding of *Saint Martin*. As Collett was known not to be too enthusiastic of pony trucks as compared with bogies, it may have been in his mind to construct 6ft 0in 4-6-0s with the larger boiler, when circumstances permitted. What *is* fairly certain is that *Saint Martin* was to pioneer the rebuilding of a number of Churchwards two-cylinder 4-6-0s in the same manner – side window cabs, later pattern screw reverse and of course smaller driving wheels. With the introduction of the 'Castle' class four-cylinder engines, some 'Stars' were displaced and these in turn displaced 'Saints' from use on the faster passenger trains, although it may be remarked that the speeded up Cheltenham Spa express (the 'Cheltenham Flyer') was at the onset handled by 'Saints' (with notable results, it might be added.) In the event the rebuilding of No 2925 in December 1924 was the only 'Saint' so treated and new construction began in December 1928 – four years later – with No 4901 *Adderley Hall* first of an initial batch of 80 engines (Lot 254). This engine was at first numbered 4900 but the plates were changed before it left the works and the number 4900 was applied to *Saint Martin* on 7 December 1928. This may have been a deliberate move on the part of Collett, who was very well aware of Great Western traditions, to indicate the continuity of design. He had attempted in 1924 to have the '47xx' named, using some former broad gauge names; the following being suggested: *Behemoth*, *Bellerophon*, *Champion*, *Dreadnought*, *Gladiator*, *Hercules*, *Mammoth*, *Plutarch*, *Romulus*, *Tantalus*, *Thunderer*, *Trafalgar*.

Around the time of the conversion of *Saint Martin* there was a scheme drawn up to fit one of these engines with a 'Star' front end and a 'Castle' cab, ie. a four-cylinder mixed traffic 4-8-0. This suggestion was soon found to be impractical however as the lower pitch of the whole engine would have caused the inside cylinders to foul the bogie.

Later in the 1920s came schemes for more 2-6-0s. In order to use the '83xx' with their altered weight distribution, on 'Blue' routes it was proposed to fit them with No 2 boilers. This project fell through however and '43xx' had to be used until the 'Manors' were built. Later there was a scheme for an unrestricted route 2-6-0 with the No 10 boiler and 17in x 26in cylinders based on '45xx' 2-6-2T but slightly bigger. In the end there came a 'Yellow' 0-6-0 – '2251' class, a little disappointing perhaps but much cheaper. These engines were ordered with 4,000 gallon tenders which went to batches of 'Halls', the '2251s' recieving tenders from withdrawn engines. This sort of thing of course makes official costing figures difficult to interpret and almost impossible to compare across companies. (It can be said fairly definitely though that GW mixed traffic engines c1950 were very much cheaper per ton than BR Standards and *vastly* cheaper than Bulleid's light pacifics, costs of which were phenomenal.)

The production 'Halls' were re-designed 'Saints', the cylinders in fact being used for renewals on 'Saints'. They were 2½ tons heavier than *Saint Martin* . The bogie wheels were 3ft 0in instead of 3ft 2in and the valve setting gave an increased valve travel, to 7¼in. Nos 5911-99 and 6900-58 had 9in piston valves in cylinders fitted with thicker valve liners. These later reverted. It was not until 1944 that any major change took place and the 260th engine (No 6959) was built with continuous frames and bolt-on cylinders with a separate smokebox saddle. These locomotives were known as 'Modified Halls' and totalled 70 engines. They had a new pattern, larger superheater giving an increase in temperature. The weight increased by an official 16cwt. No 6967 was fitted with a welded steel firebox and No 6909 had a 'Hulson' rocking grate. Several were fitted with hopper ashpans.

Later batches of the engines appeared with a new straight sided tender with framing similar to the LMS '8F' tenders built at Swindon during the war. These tenders were lined and lettered in the post-war GWR livery with bold 'G' and 'W' each side of the crest. As early as October 1942, long before the first 'Modified Hall' was built, it was suggested that a 'Hall' be fitted with an LMS boiler of the type used on the '8F' and being built at that time at Swindon for the War Department. Hawksworth wasn't too keen on this even just for a simple comparison – perhaps on the testing plant. He decided that it must be altered a little. Many alterations were made however and finally a new class of locomotive evolved and a new boiler was designed, using the LMS tooling. These very handsome locomotives were named after 'Counties' and were to be cheaper two-cylinder version of the 'Castles'. Thirteen schemes were in fact drawn up and these are tabulated overleaf for the record. (From the beginning the LMS boiler is shown as domeless with GW top feed and safety valve bonnet.)

It will be seen that the initial proposal was made before the 'Modified Halls' were begun either in finished design or actually built, the first not appearing until March 1944. It would appear that alternatives of inside Stephenson gear or outside Walschaerts gear were put forward at each revision. No doubt the outside valve gear on the '8F' 2-8-0s had invited the comparison and no doubt by running through the valve events on the setting machine or

Below:
In the mid-1920s a scheme for a '47xx' with a 'Star' four-cylinder front end was drawn up but was not a serious proposal.
R. C. Riley

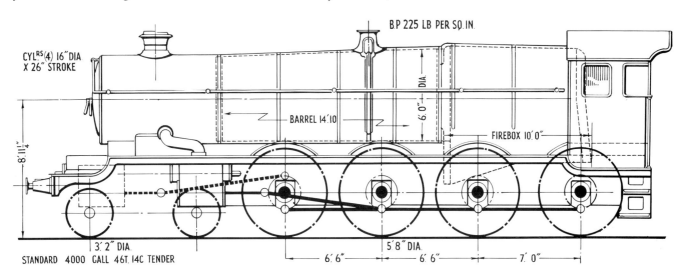

BP 225 LB PER SQ.IN.

CYLRS (4) 16" DIA X 26" STROKE

BARREL 14'10

6.0" DIA

FIREBOX 10'0"

8'11¼"

3' 2" DIA.

5'8" DIA.

6' 6" 6' 6" 7' 0"

STANDARD 4000 GALL 46T. 14C TENDER

Scheme No	Date	Driving wheels	Boiler	Notes
1	Oct 1942	6ft 0in	LMS	'Hall' with LMS boiler
2	Mar 1943	6ft 0in	LMS (modified)	
3	Mar 1943	6ft 0in	LMS (modified)	
4	Mar 1943	6ft 3in	LMS (modified)	280lb/sq in
5	Apr 1943	6ft 3in	LMS (modified)	280lb/sq in New frames and plate frame bogie
6	?	6ft 3in	S/15	Outside Walschaerts gear, raised footplate.
7	Jan 1944	6ft 3in	S/15	Outside Walschaerts gear, raised footplate
8	Feb 1944	6ft 3in	S/15	Inside valve gear, splashers
9	Feb 1944	6ft 3in	S/15	Outside valve gear, raised footplate, new tender
10	Apr 1944	6ft 3in	S/15	Inside valve gear splasher (continuous)
11	Apr 1944	6ft 3in	S/15	Outside valve gear raised footplate, gangway doors
12	May 1944	6ft 3in	S/15	Inside valve gear splasher, SS tender
13	Dec 1944	6ft 3in	OA	'9900' class Lot 354 as built

Below:
For some secondary lines further 2-6-0s were schemed but not proceeded with.

Bottom:
A light '43xx' with an S/2 boiler.

whatever, showed the GW that the advantages of the gear were outweighed by its inferiority in performance. A Layout was prepared in February 1947 for the fitting of a 'Hall' with the Walschaerts, but it was not proceeded with.

In 1946 *Garth Hall* was converted to oil burning; another ten followed. It had been planned to deal with 172 GW engines: 84 'Halls'; 25 'Castles'; and 63 '28xx'. Oil fuel depots were planned at Plymouth, Newton Abbot, Westbury, Reading, Bristol, Swindon, Didcot, Old Oak Common, Gloucester, Banbury, Severn Tunnel Junction, Newport, Cardiff, Landore and Llanelly. The scheme was a much expanded Government version of a limited Great Western exercise; in the event it was all over in 1950. The following 'Halls' were converted:

Old No	New No	Date Converted	Date Reconverted
4907	3903	May 1947	April 1950
4948	3902	May 1947	September 1948
4968	3900	May 1947	March 1949
4971	3901	May 1947	April 1949
4972	3904	May 1947	October 1948
5955	*3950	June 1946	October 1948
5976	3951	April 1947	November 1948
5986	3954	May 1947	February 1950
6949	3955	May 1947	April 1949
6953	3953	April 1947	September 1948
6957	3952	April 1947	March 1950

*Renumbered October 1946, the rest when converted.
Further information can be found in Chapter 8.

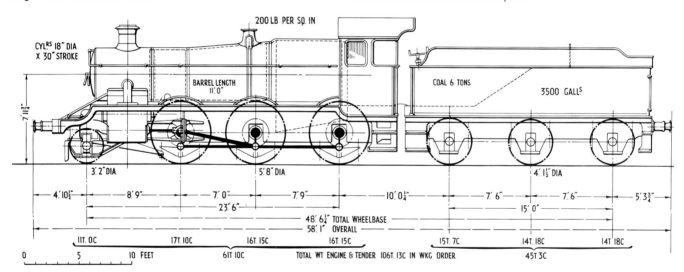

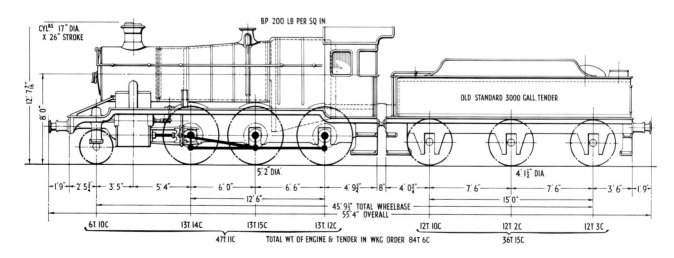

'Granges' and 'Manors'

In 1932 a new batch of 2-6-0s were built in the '93xx' series, they had a higher pitched boiler and longer frames weighing 65 ton 6 cwt full (original Nos 4301-20 were 62 ton). The new engines sported screw reverse and side window cabs, New pattern cylinders were used with outside steam pipes. One may assume that these modernised Moguls would be built as replacements for the earlier '43xx' when withdrawn but there was a great demand from the running people for bigger boilers and a leading bogie; in actual practice the '93xx' do not appear to have been anywhere near as good as the original type either. Two schemes were drawn up therefore one for a 5ft 8in 4-6-0 with a No 1 boiler for 'Red' routes and a similar engine with a smaller boiler for 'Blue' routes. Diagrams with extended No 2 and No 4 boilers were drawn up for the latter but in the event a new boiler was designed and this became the Standard No 14.

Initially the 'Red' engines were to have 'Hall' cylinders set with their centre lines 2½in above the wheel centres as had been the cylinders on the Churchward 4-6-0s. This plan was dropped however and a new design of cylinder prepared in which the piston valve centre line was an extra 2½in from the cylinder centre line. This enabled an extra amount of steam chest volume to be got into the casting and made the smaller-wheeled 'Granges', as these engines became, as free running as the 'Halls'. It was originally planned to replace 300 2-6-0s with 'Granges' and 'Manors'. In the event only 80 'Granges' and 20

'Manors' were built before the hostilities of World War 2 commenced. A further 10 'Manors' were built in 1950 but these were not classed as renewals of 2-6-0s.

There is one interesting byway in the mixed traffic engine saga on the GWR of the 1930s. Collett was not greatly interested in producing new types of locomotive unless they fitted into the basic Churchward scheme of things and could be standardised in the Works. Two Sentinel 0-4-0 100hp engines had been acquired however in 1926, one a shunter and one fitted with a vacuum brake for branch line passenger train working. The latter (No 12) was tried on the Fowey branch but found to be unsuitable and returned to the makers. Collett does therefore appear to have been prepared to give thought to more radical solutions to traction problems if the benefits had enough potential. The streamlined diesel railcars are a good case in point. The ARLE, although not the social force it was in the days of Dean, Johnson, Wainwright, Ivatt and Churchward, still met in the 1930s often though with

Below:
Scheme No 1 for the 'Red' route 4-6-0 with 5ft 8in wheels – the 'Grange' class.

Bottom:
Scheme No 2 for the 'Blue' route 4-6-0 with 5ft 8in wheels – the 'Manor' class.

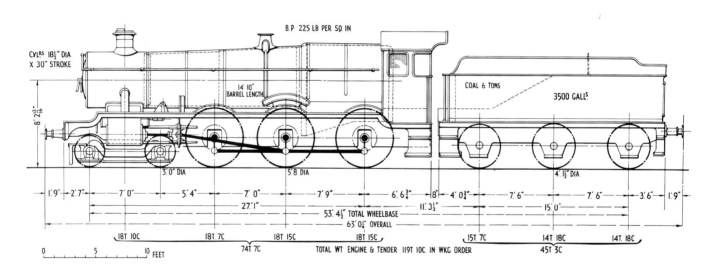

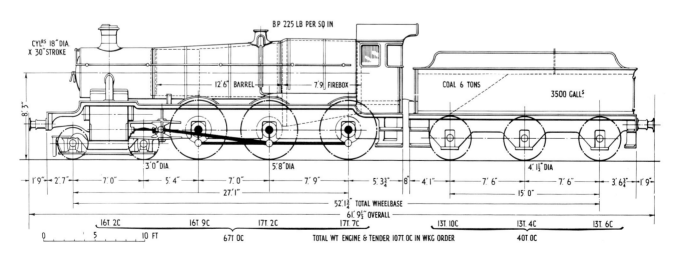

subordinates rather than the CMEs themselves. Many of them visited Belgium in 1934 to see the tests of a metre gauge Co-Co Sentinel built for the Colombian National Railways. This was one of three total adhesion locomotives with totally enclosed, nose-suspended steam engines geared to each axle. The boiler was of the 'Woolnough' water-tube type as fitted to the large LNER Sentinel steam railcars. They were designed to haul up to 200 tons on 1 in 50 gradients and tested on 1 in 28 inclines in Belgium. Speeds well over 50mph were also achieved on more favourable track.[14, 15]

Hawksworth was the GW observer in Belgium, Stanier from the LMS, Clayton from the SR and Gresley and Bulleid from the LNER were also present. The GWR later had the specification for a 600hp standard gauge Bo-Bo machine drawn up by Sentinels; the LNER actually ordered such a machine but it never materialised. Sentinel Waggon Works had considerable financial problems in the 1930s. Their technical consultant at this time, and the man behind these radical locomotives was the American, Abner Doble, one of the century's greatest innovators in regard to small steam traction units. His prototype triple expansion lorry built in 1936 by Sentinel produced performances unequalled by British lorries for a quarter of a century. No doubt the seeds of Bulleid's 'Leader' project came from this episode.

In the early 1930s the private locomotive builders were all going through a sticky patch, none more so than Beyer-Peacock who were never slow to publicise the advantages of the Beyer-Garratt articulated type. They tried to interest the GWR with diagrams of two types of heavy freight 2-8-0 + 0-8-2T and a mixed traffic 4-6-0 + 0-6-4T with 5ft 8in driving wheels. This double 'Grange' as it were was given short shrift by the GWR, but it is interesting to note that when the Iranian Government required some large standard gauge Garratts in 1936 for handling 400 ton trains up forty miles of 1 in 36 they came to Britain for advice. And where did they go? To the LMS or LNER, both Garratt users? – No. To the Southern who were interested in Garratts? – No. They went in fact to the GWR and Collett's chief running man, F. C. Hall took charge of the project. Full specifications were drawn up for a massive 4-8-2 + 2-8-4T at Swindon. The *GWR Magazine* said:

'the Great Western Railway may legitimately take a personal pride in their performance, the success of which will have depended in no small measure upon the skill and knowledge placed at the disposal of the Iranian Government by the company.'

Four of these 204 ton monsters were built and may still be in existence as part of Iran's strategic reserve in Tehran.

Right:
The Churchward mixed traffic engine finally appeared as a tender engine version of the '3150' class tank. Here is one of the earlier engines with tall safety valve bonnet and large copper-capped chimney; it is No 4388 of 1916 withdrawn in 1939, ostensibly renewed by either a 'Grange' or 'Manor'. *Real Photos (T6235)*

Below:
No 4373 in post World War 1 condition, plain unlined green and cast iron chimney. *Real Photos (W5290)*

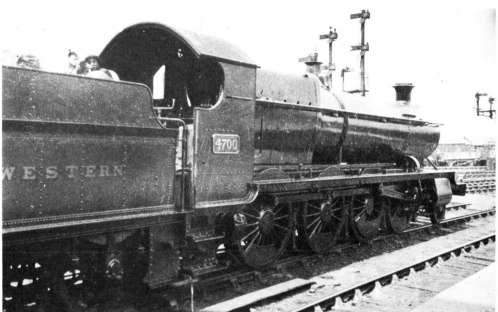

Above left:
The extra weight behind the bufferbeam on the '83xx' series is seen clearly here on No 8390; built in 1920 and altered to this condition in 1928, it reverted to '53xx' condition in 1944. *Real Photos (W5301)*

Left:
Churchward's later solution to the mainline mixed traffic engine was a lengthened '43xx'; that is into a 2-8-0 and fitted with the Standard No 1 boiler. No 4700 in a rare shot is shown here in traffic. It received a larger boiler in May 1921, having been built in this form in May 1919.
P. J. Garland collection, courtesy R. C. Riley

Below:
No 4703 on an empty stock working. The anti-vacuum valves for these engines as built were originally fitted to the outside of the steam chests and can be clearly seen. *Real Photos (R8127)*

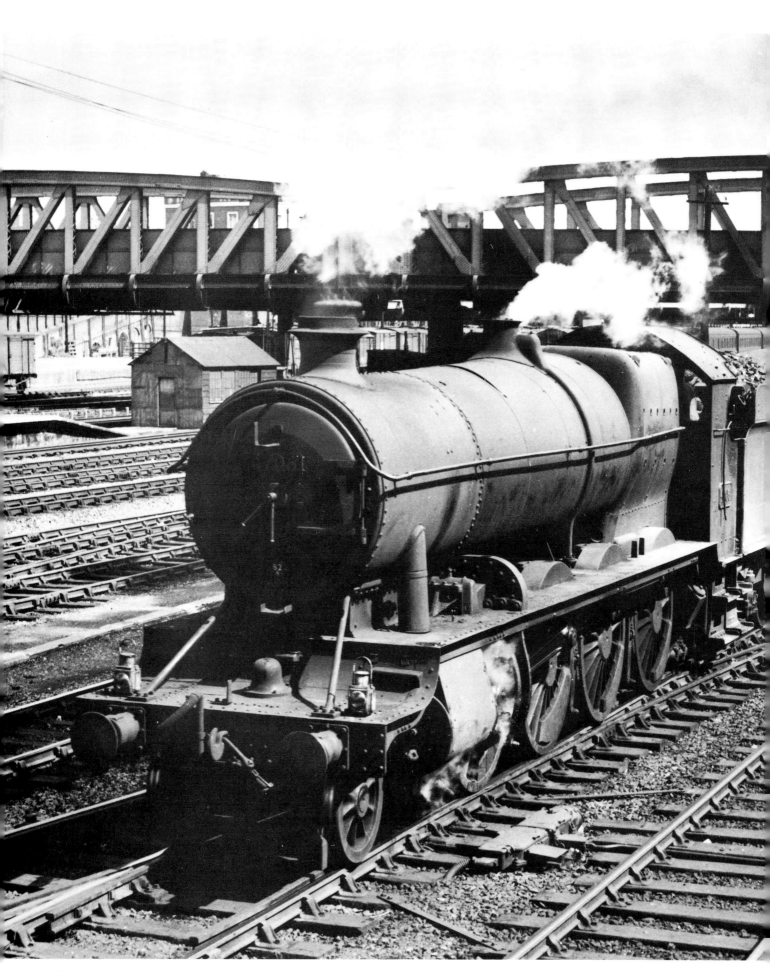

Left:
No 4706 with a down express of mainly Hawksworth stock. *R. C. Riley*

Above:
The enormous reversing lever in the cab of No 4707. The footplate was higher than on any other GW class. *R. C. Riley*

Below:
No 4704 at Old Oak Common carriage sheds. *R. C. Riley*

Top:
No 2925 *Saint Martin* before rebuilding to the prototype 'Hall'. *Real Photos (W863)*

Above:
A view of the left-hand side taken at the same time. The cast-iron chimney was particularly unsuited to the 'Saints'. *Real Photos (W864)*

Right:
No 2925 following rebuilding. Although retaining its 'Saint' numberplates, the nameplates have been altered, the letters having been spaced closer together. Brass beading has been applied to the cab windows and leading edge of the cab, but not to the splashers. *Real Photos (14212)*

Top:
Saint Martin after renumbering 4900 (in December 1928). It has had a boiler change since the previous photograph; a boiler which had previously been on an engine with outside steampipes by the look of the patches on the smokebox. It is here sporting a Collett 4,000 gallon tender. *Real Photos (W2345)*

Above:
A later photograph, having reverted to the Churchward 3,500 gallon type of tender. *Real Photos (9607)*

Left:
No 5905 *Knowsley Hall* under construction in 1931 at Swindon Works. The ATC shoe is clearly visible; fitted when built to No 4921 onward. *Real Photos (W2367)*

Left:
No 4964 *Rodwell Hall* **in Swindon stock shed awaiting return to traffic.** *Real Photos (W2369)*

Below left:
No 4971 *Stanway Hall* **ex-works fresh from the paint shop, attired in the British Railways mixed traffic livery of lined black.** *R. C. Riley*

Below:
No 6928 *Underley Hall* **outside the Weighbridge shed at Swindon Works, in full BR passenger livery with the later type of emblem.** *R. C. Riley*

Above right:
The first four 'Granges' were built with cast-iron chimneys. No 6802 *Bampton Grange* **is shown here, brand new.** *Real Photos (3945)*

Right:
No 6807 *Birchwood Grange* **on a running-in turn consisting of a 'B' set.** *(3869)*

Below right:
No 6833 *Calcot Grange* **also running in, photographed at Westbury Shed, 11 September 1937.** *R. C. Riley*

Left:
No 6866 *Morfa Grange* under construction in Swindon 'A' shop on 26 February 1939. *R. C. Riley*

Below left:
No 7808 *Cookham Manor* (now preserved) in prewar days at Bristol. *Real Photos (6340)*

Below:
No 7822 *Foxcote Manor* one of the 10 built under British Railways management in 1950, seen in the LNWR lined black livery with a small BR emblem. *Real Photos (W2342)*

Above right:
No 7313 *Freshford Manor* in unlined BR black with an 'intermediate' pattern tender and larger emblem. *Real Photos (R8086)*

Right:
No 7819 *Hinton Manor* in lined green following a limited encouragement at some regional autonomy by BR in the late 1950s. The engine has been re-draughted and is fitted with the relevant narrow chimney. *Real Photos (R8726)*

Below right:
Following Hawksworth's appointment as CME in 1941, a suggestion was made to fit a 'Hall' with a '8F' boiler (these were being constructed at Swindon for the WD at the time). This first scheme towards the 'County' class is shown here – date October 1942.

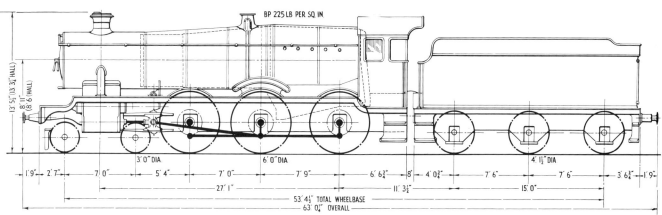

BP 225 LB PER SQ.IN.

13' 5½" (13' 3¼" HALL)
8' 11"
(8' 6 HALL)

3' 0" DIA   6' 0" DIA   4' 1½" DIA

1' 9" 2' 7"   7' 0"   5' 4"   7' 0"   7' 9"   6' 6¾" 8' 4' 0¾"   7' 6"   7' 6"   3' 6¾" 1' 9"

27' 1"   11' 3½"   15' 0"

53' 4½" TOTAL WHEELBASE
63' 0¼" OVERALL

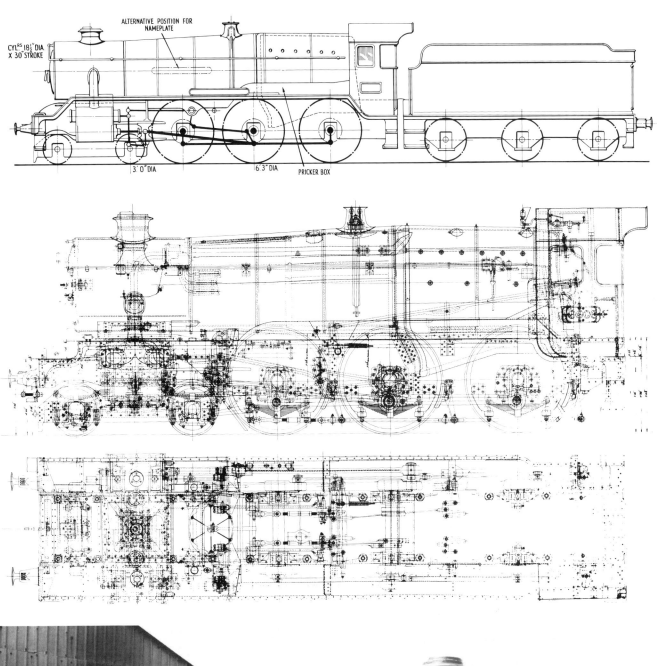

CYL^{RS} 18½" DIA
X 30" STROKE

ALTERNATIVE POSITION FOR
NAMEPLATE

3' 0" DIA   6' 3" DIA   PRICKER BOX

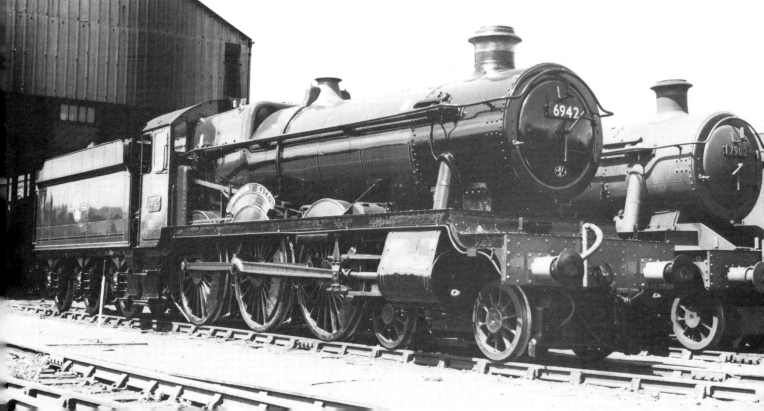

Left:
Scheme No 7 of January 1944 showing outside valve gear (Walschaerts) and a raised running plate.

Below left:
The final scheme was the 13th and this became diagram 4-6-0 A[16]. Here is the side elevation from the GA drawn by the late Ernie Nutty who did much of the design work for this class and made the original suggestion. The '99xx' number series was abandoned by an angry Hawksworth after the information had been leaked to and then published by a certain railway society.

Bottom left:
Original and Modified 'Halls' in Swindon Works Yard on 24 June 1962. The plate-frame bogie and full plate mainframes of No 7902 *Eaton Mascot Hall* can clearly be seen as can the chimney as this engine has 'Improved Draughting' whereas 6942 *Eshton Hall* has not. *R. C. Riley*

Above right:
The 'Modified Halls' appeared before the 'Counties'. Here 6965 is seen at Ebbw Junction Shed, Newport in October 1948. Nameless and without cab side windows it was named *Thirlestaine Hall* in September 1947. *R. C. Riley*

Right:
Prototype 'County' No 1000 *County of Middlesex* still carrying the experimental double chimney with which it was built. *R. C. Riley*

Below right:
The second 'County' No 1001 at Exeter St Davids in September 1946, before receiving its nameplates – *County of Bucks*. Note the front footstep unique to these GW 4-6-0s. *R. C. Riley*

Above left:
No 1026 *County of Salop* in British Railways lined black. These were very handsome engines in their single chimney form. *R. C. Riley*

Left:
No 1000 *County of Middlesex* in final condition at Swindon Works. The later double chimney did not look too good from a distance but observed close up, from a lower level they looked very impressive machines. *Real Photos (R6439)*

Below:
One of the fine 4-8-2+2-8-4 standard gauge Garratts for Iran, specifications for which were drawn up at Swindon (together with some wide-firebox 2-8-0s) under the direction of F. C. Hall, Chief Running Assistant to Collett. *Beyer-Peacock & Co*

Bottom:
The Beyer-Peacock 4-6-0+0-6-4 Garratt suggestion. Two or three would have been all that the GWR could have usefully employed, but a large class would have been needed to make economic sense.

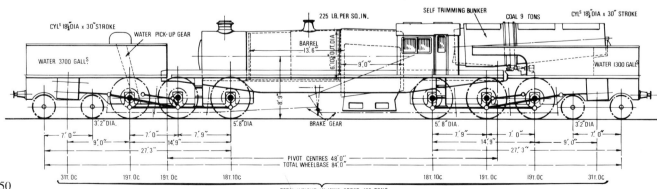

Above:
Tests in Belgium on a Co-Co
Sentinel produced a party of
famous British locomen.
Representing the GWR was F. W.
Hawksworth (10th from left); also
in the picture are Sir Nigel
Gresley and O.V.S. Bulleid (both
LNER), Stanier (LMS) and Clayton
(SR) as well as representatives of
consulting engineers and some
Continental engineers. *Author's
collection*

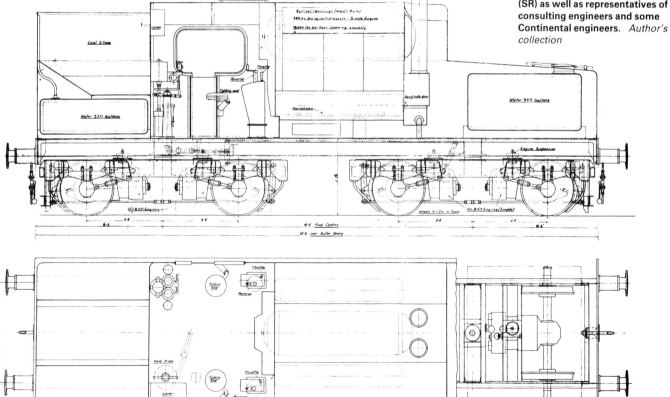

Above:
General arrangement of a Bo-Bo locomotive from a specification
drawn up for the GWR. The LNER actually ordered a machine of this
type. Such a machine would have been able to undertake the tasks
performed by the 'Manors' before the war. *Sentinel Waggon Works*

51

5
Mixed Traffic

The mixed traffic locomotive concept of the locomotive engineer quickly became the 'general utility' locomotive of the railway operating departments on many companies. Brian Reed explained this very well in 1950:[16]

'A corollary of locomotive haulage on a railway of any size is that sooner or later 'the call' comes for a general-purpose locomotive; sooner on those railways where locomotive running is largely out of the hands of the chief mechanical engineer, for it is the 'traffic' then who want a locomotive that will not only go anywhere but do anything, so that there need be no search for a motive-power unit to do some job – the first one at hand will be suitable. The idea of such a locomotive has much attraction; though here again, diesel and electric forms can give something more nearly approaching it without the inevitable tendency in steam to overdo it.

'But the desire to have it available for almost every route severely limits the axle load and weight per foot run – and so the power. Therefore it is really suitable for very few main line duties, though its inefficiency may be hidden because of the inefficiency of the other motive-power units and because of the almost complete lack of knowledge of railway mechanics on the part of railway personnel. The LMSR built hundreds of 4-6-0 general-utility locomotives of Class 5, able to travel over 70 per cent of the company's mileage. But their widespread use on main line trains over the Western, Midland and Southern Scottish divisions was perhaps the principal locomotive reason for the chronic main line unpunctuality of that system in the early postwar years. The LNER built large numbers of a 2-6-2 type which could run over only 43 per cent of the company's mileage. But the greater weight and power thus permited enabled the locomotives to take regular turns on the most exacting duties without loss of time, and enabled clearing of the most crucial sections at the expense of inability to haul an occasional train over some lightly-trafficked branch or secondary line. When the company subsequently constructed a lighter form of 4-6-0 able to run over 65 per cent of the mileage, over-loading led to their replacement on many duties, eg the 'Queen of Scots' Pullman between Leeds and Newcastle, which it was hoped they would

work, and little alleviation was given to the shortage of top-class main line power.'

This was not a problem on the Great Western Railway, four-cylinder engines were built from June 1906 to August 1950 to deal with all fast express passenger services and in some cases these engines were diagrammed to work fast freight services, usually at night. These workings were usually performed by a combination of 'Castles' and '47xx' 2-8-0s but it will be remembered that it was also a regular working of the solitary 4-6-2, No 111 *The Great Bear*, specifically the 10.45am, or 11.15am down passenger train returning with the 7.40pm or 10.5pm Bristol to Paddington fast fitted freight.

The running of goods trains at the same sort of average speeds as stopping passenger trains was possible only with the increased use of the continuous brake. It was essential that adequate brake power was available for trains to stop reliably from high speeds. It was however a slow process to introduce express goods trains, as vacuum fitted wagons could only be introduced gradually and much goods traffic was still transported by slow, loose-coupled trains. The latter, which were likely to stop at many intermediate goods stations and be divided and shunted would require much more effort in such tasks if brake connections and screw couplings had to be dealt with. There was too, the vast number of private owners' wagons running on the railway and try as they may the GWR had great difficulty in persuading the owners of such vehicles to change their habits; slow, mixed goods trains, loose-coupled and unbraked and with grease lubricated axleboxes needing regular inspection, were therefore dragged from one loop or lay-by around the system until the end of the company's existence.

The introduction of express goods trains by the GWR was in 1905 (apart from perishables such as fish and meat which were carried in braked vehicles attached to passenger trains) and over the years the number of trains and their destinations increased. Following is a table of the first of these trains and the accelerations that the use of the continuous brake brought about.

After World War 1 the number of fitted and partially fitted

From	To	Departure time		Journey time		Acceleration	
		1905	1901	1905	1909	Booked	Actual
				Hr min	Hr min	Hr min	Hr min
London	Birkenhead	9.35pm	9.35pm	11.30	9.00	2.30	2.36
London	Swansea	9.15pm	9.55pm	9.20	8.00	1.20	1.55
London	Fishguard	12.5am	12.5am	15.05	11.40	3.25	4.24
London	Wolverhampton	11.5pm	11.15pm	7.50	5.05	2.45	2.48
London	Exeter	10.38pm	10.48pm	8.52	6.00	2.52	3.24
Acton	Bristol	9.30pm	12.45am	6.00	3.22	2.38	3.02
Birkenhead	London	7.0pm	8.15pm	13.45	10.05	3.40	5.55
Plymouth	London	4.45pm	6.2pm	10.00	8.33	1.27	1.46
Wolverhampton	London	9.30pm	9.20pm	8.30	6.05	2.25	2.57
Fishguard	London	2.45pm	9.0pm	17.15	9.00	8.15	10.08
Bristol	London	8.58pm	10.20pm	5.52	4.00	1.52	3.25

freight trains increased considerably. Many of them were given unofficial nicknames and around 1930 these were collected together and published. They were soon displayed in publicity material and took on an official slant. One of the schemes started around this time by the GWR was a registered goods transit system. This service was given the name 'Green Arrow' and was soon adopted by the other companies, but the GWR had its thunder stolen somewhat when the LNER named the first of their 2-6-2 mixed traffic engines *Green Arrow*.

The following list is that given in official Great Western publicity material; the nickname often giving more than a hint of the principal goods carried. Most of these trains were hauled by 'Halls', 'Granges', Manors', '43xx' or '47xx' class engines, with the appearance of 'Castles' on some of the late-night, main line duties.

The mixed traffic engines' passenger duties usually involved hauling express trains on secondary lines and secondary trains on the main line. There were obviously many exceptions to this notably with regard to special traffic and the running of extra trains during certain – especially holiday – seasons.

Secondary lines can be considered as two types; those lines that are unable, for civil engineering reasons, to accept the largest express locomotive types, and those that can be best thought of as cross-country lines. The latter either having once been branch lines progressing into through routes due to the building of new main lines that connected with them, or purpose-built 'cut-off' lines which had become part of the route of new through services. Many cross-country services were of course inter-railway company services, sometimes straightforward complete trains and sometimes made up of various combinations of through coaches, mail vans and occasionally, catering vehicles. Inter-railway company services tended to cross at a number of locations, especially Bristol, the rather cramped Banbury, and Didcot, although at the latter place many ' trains did not actually stop.

The most notable of such services was the Aberdeen to Penzance through service, inaugurated on 3 October 1921. This service which ran every weekday left Aberdeen at 9.45am, Edinburgh 1.30pm, Newcastle-on-Tyne 4.21pm, York 6.25pm. Sheffield 7.36pm, Leicester 9.04pm, arriving at Banbury at 10pm, Oxford 10.33pm, Swindon 11.30pm, Exeter 2.46am, Torquay (Torre Station) 3.50am, Plymouth 4.25am, Newquay 7.25am, Falmouth 7.23am, St Ives 8.36am, and Penzance at 7.40am. In the reverse direction the train left Penzance at 11am, St Ives 10.25am, Falmouth 11.20am, Newquay 11.15am, Plymouth 2pm, Torquay 2.23pm, Exeter 3.27pm, Swindon 6.15pm, Oxford 7.7pm Banbury 7.42pm arriving at Leicester at 8.38pm, Sheffield 10.04pm, York 11.15pm, Newcastle-on-Tyne 1.20am, Edinburgh 4.05am and Aberdeen at 7.40am. This was the longest through train service in the British Isles, viz, 785 miles. The service was maintained by the following stock: (i) Through Aberdeen–Penzance, brake composite coach (North British and Great Western stock alternately). (ii) Through York-Penzance, brake third (Great Central stock). (iii) York-Swindon, brake first; composite dining-car and open third (North Eastern and Great Western stock alternately). At Swindon the Aberdeen-York-Penzance coaches were attached to a Great Western through express to Penzance, with sleeping cars.

After the 1923 Grouping, the GWR and LNER continued the service until the beginning of World War 2 in 1939.

Between York and Swindon these through coaches ran coupled to the postal train between those two centres; this train continued to run after World War 2.

Time	Train	Name
1.05am	Acton to Bristol	The High Flyer
7.40pm	Acton to Cardiff	The Early Bird
9.25pm	Acton to Llanelly	The Leek
3.40am	Banbury Jc to Bristol	The Competitor
2.10am	Basingstoke to Wolverhampton	The Cherbourg
9.35pm	Basingstoke to Wolverhampton (Basingstoke, Birmingham, Crewe)	The BBC
3.55pm	Birkenhead to Smithfield	The Meat
6.05pm	Birkenhead to Pontypool Rd	The Feeder
8.20pm	Birkenhead to Paddington	The General
9.05pm	Birkenhead to Cardiff	The Mersey
10.50pm	Birkenhead to Bordesley Jc	The Birmingham Market
11.35pm	Birkenhead to Oswestry	The Cambrian Pioneer
11.00pm	Birmingham to Paddington	The Pedlar
9.10pm	Bordesley Jc to Birkenhead	The Shipper
10.10pm	Bordesley Jc to Swansea	The Hardware
6.50pm	Bristol to Birkenhead	The Farmer's Boy
7.40pm	Bristol to Paddington	The 'Bacca'
9.20pm	Bristol to Wolverthampton	The Western Docker
10.05pm	Bristol to Leamington	Spa
10.05pm	Bristol to Paddington	The Cocoa
10.55pm	Bristol to Laira	The Drake
12.25am	Bristol to Carmarthen Jc	The Bristolian
3.50pm	Cardiff to Hanwell Br. Sdgs.	The Stock
9.45pm	Cardiff to Saltney	The Spud
11.10pm	Cardiff to Paddington	The Ironmonger
12.55am	Cardiff to Swansea	Port to Port
7.30pm	Carmarthen to Paddington	The Up Welshman
8.35pm	Carmarthen to Bristol	The Open
11.00am	Exeter to Pontypool Rd.	The Ponty
4.00pm	Exeter to Old Oak Common	The Flying Pig
12.05am	Gloucester to Cardiff	The Bacon
7.50pm	Gloucester to Paddington	The Cotswold
11.00pm	Handsworth to Acton	The Queen's Head
8.20pm	Kidderminster to Paddington	The Carpet
7.45pm	Manchester to Bristol	The 'Mon'
8.25pm	Manchester to Wolverhampton	The Early Riser
4.58pm	Marazion to Bristol	The Tre Pol and Pen Flyer
10.25pm	Margam to Bordesley	The Tinman
5.30pm	Newton Abbot to Paddington	The Hackney
9.32pm	Old Oak Common to Penzance	The Cornishman
8.05pm	Paddington to Bristol	The Shopper
9.10pm	Paddington to Birkenhead	Northern Flash
9.35pm	Paddington to Carmarthen Jc	The Welshman
10.10pm	Paddington to Laira	The Tamar
10.30pm	Paddington to Cardiff	South Wales Borderer
10.50pm	Paddington to Weymouth	The Jersey
11.05pm	Paddington to Wolverhampton	The Hampton
11.15pm	Paddington to Bristol	The Western General
11.35pm	Paddington to Newton Abbot	The Devonshireman
12.05am	Paddington to Worcester	The Sauce
12.15am	Paddington to Fishguard	Irishman
12.30am	Paddington to Bristol	The Mopper Up
12.10am	Park Royal to Stourbridge Jc	The Stour
2.50pm	Penzance to Paddington	The Searchlight
7.20pm	Penzance to Plymouth	The Pasty
5.40am	Pontypool Rd. to Newton Abbot	The Laira
10.30pm	Reading to Laira	The Biscuit
11.40pm	Southall to Crewe	The Grocer
3.50pm	Swindon to Tavistock Jc	The Rasher
7.10pm	Victoria Basin to Basingstoke	The Cargo
4.20am	Westbury to Wolverhampton	The Moonraker
7.35pm	Westbury to Manchester	The Lancashire Lad
9.55pm	Westbury to Penzance	Western Flash
10.50pm	Westbury to Pontypool Rd	The Northern
7.22pm	West Drayton to Wolverhampton	The Drayton
6.35pm	Weymouth to Paddington	The Up Jersey
1.30pm	Wolverhampton to Basingstoke	The Southern Docker
2.10am	Wolverhampton to Basingstoke	The Southerner
2.45am	Wolverhampton to Birkenhead	The Northern Docker
4.00am	Wolverhampton to Crewe	The Northern Exchange
8.15pm	Wolverhampton to Paddington	The Racer
10.15pm	Wolverhampton to Westbury	The Crosser
12.45am	Wolverhampton to Birkenhead	The Flying Skipper
6.45pm	Worcester to Cardiff	The Worcester Fruit
8.35pm	Worcester to Crewe	The 'Sparagras'

One of the cross-country services that provided a regular and well patronised service was the Cardiff to Portsmouth service. Great Western mixed traffic engines could be seen on Southern metals when working these trains. ''Halls'' were regular engines, together with the '43xx' 2-6-0s and earlier engines used for mixed traffic work such as the 5ft 8in 4-4-0 'Bulldogs'. Southern locomotives were to be seen on some of these trains, usually 'U' class 2-6-0s, and the rolling stock was likewise used from both companies. Through services were first introduced in 1896 and there were five trains each way each weekday (two on Sundays) until 6 May 1968 when the service was reduced. These trains in steam days were the only regular exceptions to Portsmouth Harbour's all-electric services. There were also through services by this route from South Wales to both Brighton and Bournemouth.

Another through service that lasted only until World War 2, was that from Barry (South Wales) to Newcastle which had been introduced to facilitate the exchange of ships' crews between South Wales and Tyneside. The Barry worked the train to Cardiff and the GW took over as far as Banbury where the GC took charge to York, the journey thereafter being in the hands of the North Eastern. After World War 1 the service was extended to Swansea and a through coach from Cardiff to Hull was added. In the early days 2-4-0s ran the service due to the small turntable at Banbury but later '43xx' were used and finally 'Manors' which were the largest engines allowed on the Banbury and Cheltenham Railway (a 'blue' route).

Other cross-country train services involving inter-railway working were Bournemouth West to Manchester and Birkenhead; and Bournemouth West to Newcastle, with through coaches for Bradford and Manchester. Both of these trains used the GW line from Basingstoke to Reading and LSWR locomotives (later SR) worked through to Oxford. The GW also ran onto the South Eastern at Reading and thence to Redhill and finally on to coastal towns of the south east (Folkstone, Dover and Deal) or the south 'Brighton'). Through trains also ran via the West London Railway and West London Extension Railway to Longhedge Junction and Herne Hill where very colourful trains (in pre-grouping days) were made up of SE&CR, Midland, LNWR and Great Western stock. The latter worked from Birkenhead to Deal. Through coaches also worked from the south west to Glasgow via the LNWR west coast main line, and Bristol to Shrewsbury through the Severn Tunnel.

The Great Western main line west of Plymouth was the home of numbers of mixed traffic engines, indeed for many years no four-cylinder engines were seen west of the Royal Albert Bridge (the 'Kings' of course never were), until the 'Cornish Riviera Limited' was allowed a 'Castle'. In earlier days 'Duke' class 4-4-0s were used west of Newton on Paddington to Penzance expresses, but with the introduction of non-stop running to Plymouth, they were used only west of that city. The introduction of the '43xx' 2-6-0s saw those used, even on the 'Limited', in Cornwall. The Cornish main line was one of the most interesting parts of the whole Great Western system and very difficult to operate, especially during the holiday season. The route is a succession of extremely steep inclines, many on very sharp curves, the latter severely limiting any fast downhill locomotive work. If I may introduce an Irishism, the 'Granges' were the 'Kings' of Cornwall. The need for crisp accelerations away from the numerous station stops, many on the banks, was met perfectly by the 'Granges' and Hawksworth's 'Counties' were also known for some excellent work. In British Railways' days the standard Class 7 'Britannia' pacifics were tried but were not universally popular and did not become permanent residents.

An important secondary line was that to Weymouth where connections were made to Channel Island steamers. Churchward's 'County' class 4-4-0s were used on this line until 1931 when 21 of the 30 engines were withdrawn, being replaced by 'Hall' class

W2353

engines of which 39 were delivered in that year. There is a severe climb out of Weymouth where the railway climbs nearly 400ft in less than five miles to the summit at Bincombe Tunnel where there is a signalbox. 'Halls' were the rule on the Weymouth trains with the occasional 'Castle' on the 'Channel Island Boat Express'. The Southern Railway also ran trains into Weymouth and it was interesting to compare the GW engines and Bulleid's light pacifics in their abilities to start and accelerate their trains and also climb the bank without slipping, a notorious failing of these Southern engines in spite of the ballyhoo surrounding them.

On 8 June 1949, No 6822 *Manton Grange* underwent clearance tests between Exeter Central and Templecombe, but was found to be too wide for satisfactory use on the Southern main line.

The 'Manor' class came into their own on the secondary lines of Wales; the Cambrian main line, the 'Manchester & Milford Railway' from Aberystwyth to Carmarthen, and the line from Ruabon to Barmouth along the valley of the Dee. This latter line ran through beautiful scenery through Llangollen, Corwen and Bala Junction down to Dolgelley where it made an end on connection with the Cambrian system. It was made up of four separate railway companies, all worked by the GWR but not finally absorbed into that concern until 1896. This route with its sharp and frequent curves and long, heavy gradients was worked by larger locomotives than those allowed on the Cambrian until that line was upgraded in World War 2. Although there were through coaches from Paddington, Birmingham and Birkenhead to Pwllheli during the summer months, regular trains on the line were usually made up of non-corridor stock for the 2½hr journey from Ruabon to Barmouth until well into the 1920s. Indeed some of the last GW four-wheeled stock was used on local trains on the line.

The running of cross-country trains may be considered of little importance; train working however is very complex and a delay incurred at one place on the system, can jeopardise the working of the whole Line. A very good example of this interraction was given by Mr F. R. Potter, Operating Assistant to the Superintendent of the Line, in a paper to the Great Western Railway (London) Lecture and Debating Society in 1930.

'The 4.30pm Penzance-Crewe, when late reacts on the 3.30pm Shrewsbury-Welshpool which reacts on the 2.45am Whitchurch-Aberystwyth which reacts on the 7.00am Aberystwyth-Carmarthen which reacts on the 7.50am Pembroke Dock-Paddington which reacts on the 12.20pm Cardiff-Brighton delaying the 12.30pm Paddington-Weymouth (at Westbury) which reacts on the 12.30pm Cardiff-Pontypool Road-Birmingham which delays the 8.45am Plymouth-Crewe (at Pontypool Road).'

Above:
No 6913 *Levens Hall* **passes Burlescombe as it storms the 1 in 115 climb to Whiteball Summit with an up goods of 57 vans, on 17th June 1959.** *J. F. Loader*

Left:
No 4981 *Abberley Hall* **and pannier tank No 5713 climb the 1 in 50 out of Fishguard with the 3.35pm Class C Fishguard Harbour to Paddington freight on 25 June 1959.** *J. F. Aylard*

Top right:
No 5917 *Westminster Hall* **on a long train of coal wagons.** *R. C. Riley*

Above right:
No 5958 *Knolton Hall* **running through Challow with a train of milk tank wagons.** *R. C. Riley*

Right:
No 7907 *Hart Hall* **heading south from Bristol past Bedminster Park with a mixed freight including china clay empties.**

Left:
No 7917 *North Aston Hall*
R. C. Riley

Below left:
No 6800 *Arlington Grange* shunting at Truro. R. C. Riley

Bottom left:
No 6825 *Llanvair Grange* trundles over the Royal Albert Bridge at the regulation 15 mph on 28 April 1962. Brian Haresnape

Right:
No 6873 *Caradoc Grange* climbs purposefully up the 1 in 60 out of Truro station with the down 'Cornish Riviera Express' on 19 May 1959. Normally a diesel-hydraulic turn, the train was nearly ½-hour late due to diesel locomotive failure.
M. Mensing

Below:
No 6875 *Hindford Grange* passes Long Rock depot, Penzance, on 11 May 1955 with the 1.55pm Penzance-Plymouth.
M. Mensing

Above:
No 6828 *Trellech Grange* with a china clay train near Plymouth.
R. C. Riley

Right:
No 6826 *Nannerth Grange* runs through Plymouth North Road with a train of concrete sleepers.
R. C. Riley

Top:
No 7810 *Draycott Manor* of
Shrewsbury shed rattles through
Birmingham Snow Hill with an up
class H freight on 13 September
1953. *R. C. Riley*

Above:
No 5969 *Honington Hall* in
Cornish china clay country with
the Newquay portion of the 9.30
am ex-Paddington at St. Dennis
Junction on 11 July 1955.
R. C. Riley

Right:
Glorious Devon. No 7924
***Thornycroft Hall* leaving Dawlish**
with the 1.30pm Bristol-Penzance
on 17 April 1960. *J. C. Beckett*

Above:
No 4970 *Sketty Hall* entering Exeter St Davids from Taunton with a through train in 1935. *D. E. H. Box*

Right:
No 6868 *Penrhos Grange* heading westward beside the sea wall at Teignmouth with an 'H' headcode freight. *R. C. Riley*

Below right:
In the 1950s some 'Manors' were sent to the West Country for piloting duties on the South Devon banks. Here No 7814 *Fringford Manor* is seen at the head of a 'King'-powered up Cornish express climbing Hemerdon bank in the summer of 1953. *R. Russell*

On the Weymouth line

Right:
No 7924 *Thornycroft Hall* seen shortly after leaving Yeovil (Pen Mill) with the 11.10 am Wolverhampton-Weymouth made up of ex-LNER Gresley stock. The date is 17 August **1963.** *B. J. Ashworth*

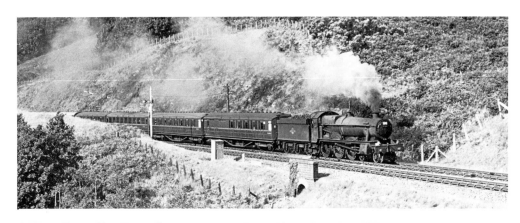

Below right:
No 5978 *Bodinnick Hall* pauses at Maiden Newton with a Yeovil stopping train, while 2-6-2T No 4507 waits in the bay with the Bridport branch connection. *C. P. Boocock*

Below:
No 4957 *Postlip Hall* storms up the Upwey Bank out of Weymouth with the 11.12 to Paddington on 23 July 1960 supposedly banked by BR Class 5 No 73017 although the latter is blowing off rather than working very hard. Churchward's 'County' 4-4-0s took very heavy loads up this bank unassisted. *Derek Cross*

'Counties' at the extremities-

Right:
About to leave for Plymouth and Paddington in July 1953 is No 1023 *County of Oxford* standing in Penzance station. *P. L. Melvill*

Below:
At Chester General on 20 May 1961 is No 1026 *County of Salop*, seen here departing with a Birkenhead to Paddington express. *A. H. Bryant*

Right:
No 7826 *Longworth Manor* **leaves the remote Strata Florida with the 10.40am from Carmarthen to Aberystwyth, passing a non-functioning starting signal. No 7828** *Odney Manor* **waits the signal to re-start with the 12 noon from Aberystwyth on 7 September 1963.** *A. A. Vickers*

Below:
No 7812 *Erlestoke Manor* **departs from Aberystwyth on 20 September 1965 with a portion of the 'Cambrian Coast Express'.** *M. S. Welch*

Left:
No 7815 *Fritwell Manor* **at speed between Clarbeston Road and Clynderwen with through coaches from Milford Haven to Paddington.** *Ian Allan Library*

Right:
No 7808 *Cookham Manor* **clings to the Central Wales coastline as it heads north for Barmouth with a train from Birmingham on 22 July 1961.** *T. A. Chadwick*

Left:
No 7827 *Lydham Manor* crossing Barmouth Bridge with a Birkenhead express on 24 May 1955. *P. H. Wells*

On the Cambrian Railway Main Line-

Below left:
The up 'Cambrian Coast Express' between Dovey Junction and Machynlleth on 17 May 1957 headed by No 7802 *Bradley Manor*. The stock is in BR 'blood and custard' and the locomotive in plain black livery. *D. S. Fish*

Above right:
No 7810 *Draycott Manor* running through Talerddig station with the 2.30pm Aberystwyth-Oswestry on 29 July 1959. Both lines through this station were signalled in the down direction in order to facilitate the running of banking engines back to Machynlleth.
R. O. Tuck

Right:
No 7821 *Ditcheat Manor* climbing Talerddig Bank with the 10.45am Aberystwyth-Manchester Piccadilly on 29 August 1964.
G. T. Robinson

Below:
No 7810 *Draycott Manor* with an Aberystwyth train at Welshpool on 20 June 1963. *R. Hewitt*

Above:
No 7800 *Torquay Manor* at Llanymynech on the 9.45am Whitchurch-Aberystwyth on 28 July 1962. The lines to the right are those of the Shropshire & Montgomeryshire Railway.
L. Sandler

Right:
No 1005 *County of Devon* blasts its way to Church Stretton with a Manchester-Plymouth express on 30 March 1963. *G. England*

Below right:
Under the wires. No 7809 *Childrey Manor* leaves Crewe with the 7.50pm to Whitchurch on 29 June 1959 with progress very advanced on the WCML electrification. *R. O. Tuck*

Above left:
No 7824 *Iford Manor* **and 7817** *Garsington Manor* **head the Royal Train out of Banbury on 24 May 1962.** *T. J. Edgington*

Left:
Unusual operation. No 4907 *Broughton Hall* **at Bicester North with the slip coach from the 5.10am Paddington-Wolverhampton which it has collected from the through road in order to attach it to its own train – the 4.34pm Paddington-Wolverhampton on 31 May 1960** *M. Mensing*

Below:
Crossing the River Wye at Backney is No 7800 *Torquay Manor* **with the 16.00 Gloucester-Hereford on 22 June 1964.** *B. J. Ashworth*

Left:
The 8.00am Plymouth-Liverpool leaving Weston-super-Mare in the charge of No 1026 *County of Salop*. *W. N. Lockett*

Below left:
Bristol, July 1956. A West to North special takes the avoiding line headed by a 'Hall' class 4-6-0. Bath Road shed is in the background. *D. A. Pilkington*

Below:
No 7820 *Dinmore Manor* storms out of Ledbury on the 12.05pm from Hereford for Paddington on 15 March 1962. *A. A. Vickers*

Above right:
No 6979 *Helperley Hall* and ex-SR No 30790 *Sir Villiers* at Leicester Central station on 7 August 1954. *H. A. Gamble*

Right:
The 5.20pm Leicester-Woodford arriving at Whetstone behind No 6911 *Holker Hall* on 6 July 1961. This is the return engine working off the 11.16am Bournemouth-York train. *M. Mitchell*

Below right:
Bournemouth Central on 24 August 1963 with the 11.36 Bournemouth-Derby awaiting department headed by No 6851 *Hurst Grange*. *R. A. Panting*

Above:
Following a landslip between Lavington and Patney, a number of Western Region expresses were re-routed via Reading, Basingstoke, Exeter Central and Okehampton to Plymouth. Here No 6973 *Bricklehampton Hall* enters Exeter Central with the 8.25am Paddington-Penzance on 26 August 1961. *H. Ball*

Below:
On 22 June 1962 No 7808 *Cookham Manor* rounds the curve into Redhill (SR) with the 10.35am (Saturdays only) Birmingham Snow Hill to Hastings. *G. D. King*

Right:
No 7829 *Ramsbury Manor* moving its empty stock out of Redhill after working the 06.50 from Reading on 28 August 1964. *G. D. King*

Above:
The two remaining steam turns at Stratford-on-Avon on 2 March 1963.
No 6817 *Gwenddwr Grange* is leaving with the 8.30am to Birmingham
Snow Hill while Collett 0-6-0 No 2211 prepares to take the 8.43am to
Leamington Spa. *G. England*

Below:
On a cold and snowy day in December 1964 a very dirty No 7829
Ramsbury Manor leaves Betchworth with the 11.35 Redhill-Reading
train. *Brian Stephenson*

6
Shop, Shed and Road

The factors that make for successful locomotive design centre around men and materials as much as drawing office acumen and workshop skill. Good water for locomotives is essential and Churchward had a number of water softening plants installed and water troughs laid down at regular intervals on the main lines. In 1906 the GWR locomotives used 9 million tons of water and this all cost money. For example the 'Desrumaux' softening plant at Goring dealt with 20,000 gallons per hour at a cost of ½d per 1,000 gallons. Hardness in water would scale up in locomotive boilers and reduce conductivity (water-side) drastically this could cause fire-side metal temperatures to rise to dangerous levels and increase maintenance and renewal requirements. Soluble salts in water can cause 'priming' even in small quantities and chemicals used for softening must not aggravate this effect.

The following is a list of water troughs installed and the dates opened:

Name	Between	Date	Length (yd)
Aldermaston	Aldermaston & Midgham	June 1904	560
Charlbury	Charlbury & Ascott-under-Wychwood	June 1906	560
Chipping Sodbury	Badminton & Chipping Sodbury	June 1903	524
Creech	Cogload Jcn & Creech Jen	Feb 1902	560
Denham Joint	Denham and Ruislip & Ickenham	Sept 1906	560
Exminster	Exminster & Starcross	June 1904	560
Ferryside	Ferryside & Carmarthen Jcn	July 1907	620
Goring: main line	Pangbourne & Goring and Streatley	Oct 1895	620
Goring: relief	Pangbourne & Goring and Streatley	June 1898	620
Keynsham	Keynsham & Fox's Wood	June 1899	620
King's Sutton	Aynho & King's Sutton	Oct 1906	560
Lapworth	Hatton & Rowington Jcn	Oct 1899	560
Ludlow Joint	Bromfield & Ludlow	April 1896	613
Severn Tunnel	Undy Crossing & Magor	Oct 1905	560
Westbury	Fairwood Jcn & Clink Rd Jcn	June 1904	553 Down 495 Up

Some of these troughs became known by other names but those given are GWR official ones of c1908.

In later years (ie Western Region, BR) areas notorious for bad water such as Wolverhampton, had locomotives fitted with 'Afloc' feed water treatment. This was a fairly simple arrangement whereby chemical briquettes were added to tender feed water via a feeder tube which extended into the tender tank and had holes for circulation of water and mixing with chemical. This arrangement allowed the period between boiler washouts to be extended, and a reduced volume of blowdown to be carried out, intermittently instead of continuously as with some other systems.

Test results in Chapter 7 show that in controlled conditions how different grades of coal affect steaming capacity; on the road then it is the experience and skill of the fireman that counts above all else. Some notes on the correct approach to firing were given in a GWR booklet, *Fuel Efficiency on the Footplate* prepared in 1945. A few are reproduced here:

'**Making up the Fire** – To prepare the fire, it should be spread evenly over the entire grate, and a few shovels of lump coal sprinkled over the fire to start it burning vigorously. The dampers should be opened and the blower applied sufficiently to promote proper combustion.

'Freshly applied coal should be left to burn up before more is added. The lumps of coal should be broken so that the largest put on the grate is about twice the size of a man's fist. This exposes to the action of the fire a greater surface than if much larger lumps were used.

'The fire should now be built up by adding a small quantity of coal at a time, any holes which may form being carefully filled. If a large quantity of coal is fired to the centre of the grate dense volumes of smoke will be produced. This is to be avoided at all times. Firing should continue at intervals, giving each charge of coal time to ignite properly before introducing more, until a bed of fire, well alight and suitable for the class of train to be worked, is obtained.

'**On the Road** – The art of firing is to regulate the fire and height of water according to the work to be performed and to have full boiler pressure when it is required, without unnecessary blowing-off. The fireman should realise that his aim must always be to obtain the maximum amount of heat from every pound of coal fired. He should anticipate the requirements of the road and manage the fire and injectors accordingly, so that steam is available for gradients, but not wasted when standing or running downhill.

'No coal should be added to the fire when the regulator is closed. When starting from a dead stop, firing should not recommence until the driver has notched-up.

'Blowing-off from the safety valve causes a serious waste of fuel. When an engine with a heavy train is on a rising gradient and is showing just a "white feather" at the safety valves, this is a sign of a capable fireman who is "firing to the road". At other times when full pressure is not necessary, blowing-off is a sign of bad judgement.

'When a fireman hands an engine over to another fireman, he should leave it in a condition such as he would wish to find it.

'Towards the end of the run, prior to disposal of an engine, the fire should be levelled in the box, and worked down as low as possible to avoid coming on the Shed with a large amount of unburned coal on the grate. Experience will soon teach a fireman the best time to commence working the fire down, but the aim should be to run on to the shed with the fire as low as possible'.

'With a grate having the front bars sloping and the hind bars level ('28xx', '29xx', '47xx', '49xx', 68xx', '40xx', '50xx', '60xx' classes) the coal should be fired far enough forward to avoid the front portion of the fire becoming thin, at the same time the fire on the level portion should be kept much thicker than that at the front end of the grate. The fire should never be too thick under the brick arch as this would badly affect the steaming of the boiler.

'A heap of fire just inside the firehole door should be avoided, as it interferes with the feeding of coal to the front of the fire and leads to coal being thrown on the brick arch.

'The rule for a fireman to observe is to fire "little and often". If coal is fired in large quantities dense volumes of smoke will be produced. This is wasteful and must be avoided at all times.'

In better days the more important main line locomotives were always supplied with bituminous coal from Ebbw Vale. This was *not* 'Welsh steam coal' which would have been useless for locomotive work and was used in ships where a constant, steady draught was available. Ebbw Vale coal was not used particularly because of its chemical qualities but because of its physical ones. It was particularly adapted to the centre or 'Haycock' fire which was the one best suited to the long fireboxes in Churchward's standard boilers. Although GW engines adapted to other coals, some classes effortlessly, for the economical output of relatively high powers for long periods of time this Ebbw Vale coal was the fuel around which the engines were designed.

The running department was a very complex organisation and the work at engine sheds very complicated, as explained by T. J. Tarrant to the Swindon Engineering Society in 1949:[17]

'Engines used on shunting or local trains return to the depot after completion of the turn, but engines on through passenger and freight trains on reaching destinations go to the nearest locomotive depot, and after servicing should work a train back in the direction of its home depot. The engine working schedules are framed with this object, but the schedules become broken down from time to time, due to various reasons, and engines are sometimes away from home several days. It has been stated simply that the prime duty of a locomotive shed foreman is to supply at the correct time an engine of the required class in good condition, properly serviced, and manned by men competent to work the train. The performance of that duty, however, is far from simple. To begin with, it must be remembered that the locomotive shed is operating 24 hours a day, every day of the year. The shed foreman has assistant foremen to cover the period when he is not on duty. These supervisors in order to ensure that each engine leaves shed at the appointed time have to keep a constant watch on all engines coming to shed, and the servicing operations, ie firedropping, ashpan cleaning, smokebox and tube cleaning, coaling, repairs, lighting-up, and steam raising, and preparation for the next trip. At the larger sheds with 100 or more engines being turned off each 24 hours, this is a job of some magnitude. In addition, these foremen have to see that footplate staff are properly booked up for commencing duty at the correct time to suit the various turns. To describe in more detail the servicing operations, let us consider an engine just arriving at shed. The driver and fireman will leave the engine after making it secure on the coal stage road. Making an engine secure means putting the engine in mid-gear, opening the cylinder cocks, applying the hand brake and making sure that there is plenty of water in the boiler. The driver and fireman then proceed to the Time Office to book off duty, first making a report of any known defects to the engine, and making out what is known as the Daily Record. This record is a tabulated sheet of paper on which he records all that has been done during the turn of duty with the engine. This record after checking is forwarded to the Divisional Office and finally to Swindon to the Statistical Section, where it is used for many purposes, including the compilation of engine mileage statistics.'

Mr Tarrant then goes through a detailed description of the

cleaning of smokebox and tubes, firedropping, coaling and fire lighting. Every 7-14 days the boiler was washed out; the standard system on the GWR was to wash out with hot water supplied from the shed stationary boiler.

Repairs were carried out at sheds if and when necessary, a driver having to fill in a 'Repairs' report card after every trip. There were other repairs carried out on a preventive maintenance basis following periodic examinations. Boilers were examined by the Divisional Boiler Inspector as follows:

160lb/sq in and less	– 6 months
165-180lb/sq in inclusive	– 4 months
Above 180lb/sq in	– 2 months

Some other components were examined as detailed below:

Examinations after one month: ATC apparatus, water gauge frames, springs, brake gear, crossheads, motion bar bolts, wheels and tyres, crank axles, injectors, lubrication.
After two months: Connecting and coupling rods, brake gear, smokebox with all fittings, water scoop.
After four months: Axleboxes, piston valves, most classes, slide valves on superheated engines.
After six months: Slide valves non-superheated engines.
After eight months: Pistons and cylinders, most classes.
After twelve months: Safety valves.

In 1933 the GWR had 14 booked schedules for locomotives that involved a daily mileage exceeding 300. The majority were rostered to 'Castles' or 'Stars' but four were to two cylinder 4-6-0s as follows:

Engine Type	Service			Hours	Miles
'29xx'	Swindon	dep	12.42am		
	Paddington	arr	2.40am		
		dep	4.30am		
	Swindon	arr	8.35am		
		dep	9.03am		
	Cardiff	arr	11.16am		
		dep	1.30pm		
	Swindon	arr	5.48pm	17	330
'49xx'	Wolverhampton	dep	7.10am		
	Birmingham	arr	7.40am		
		dep	8.33am		
	Chester	arr	10.41am		
		dep	12.20pm		
	Wolverhampton	arr	3.08pm		
		dep	5.30pm		
	Oxford	arr	7.43pm		
		dep	9.08pm		
	Wolverhampton	arr	11.16pm	16	325
'49xx'	Wolverhampton	dep	7.25am		
	Taunton	arr	12.08pm		
		dep	6.35pm		
	Wolverhampton	arr	11.47pm	16¼	315
'49xx'	Chester	dep	8.35am		
	Oxford	arr	12.21pm		
		dep	1.44am		
	Chester	arr	5.35pm	9	301

Whatever figures are produced, whatever erudite arguments made and however much special pleading promoted, in the final analysis it is the men on the footplate whose opinion is what really counts. And if they have wide experience on other companies' or regions' machines then they must be listened to.

In his first book of footplate memories *Drawn by Steam*, Colin Jacks[18] tells of his years at Tyseley where he fired all the standard Great Western engines. He also had experience of most of the

LMS equivalents, Black 5s, '8Fs', 'Jubilees', 'Patriots' and 'Rebuilt Scots', and regarded the GW types to have the edge, at least. In the case of the BR types it was no contest the latter types being regarded as very poor.

Of the Great Western classes, the one that always comes top of the list for mixed traffic work, indeed for anything other than crack expresses is the 'Grange' class. It is a great pity that one at least wasn't saved from the cutter's torch but they do seem, when all the stories and reminiscences are assembled together, from footplatemen, inspectors, enthusiasts and passengers, the most versatile of all British class 5 4-6-0 locomotives. Harold Gasson summed up the footplate view admirably:

'As a replacement for the ageing '43xx' class, the design of the "Grange" was a masterpiece. It embodied all the standard parts of the locomotive that it was succeeding, with the "Hall" boiler . . . It was in fact, a "Hall" with smaller wheels and had the edge over the "Hall" for all-out power. At first glance it was difficult to see the difference between the two locomotives. [The real difference of course was the cylinder casting.] However the "Hall" frame was straight, all the way from the smokebox to the front portion of the cab, but the "Grange" frame dipped behind the cylinders before carrying on to the cab. To see that slight difference, brought a feeling of joy in my heart. We had nothing against the "Hall" class, as they were a good engine, capable of any task, but the "Grange" was something special. They had a gentleness about them, a tolerance, an air of tranquility that would forgive any transgression on the part of a ham-fisted driver or inexperienced fireman. They were one of the most loved engines on the Great Western, being the firemans' dream engine and the drivers' home from home.

'Climbing into the cab of a "Grange" gave one the feeling that it was to be the perfect day. No matter the weather, the load, the poor coal, or any other factors. One knew that there would be plenty of steam, a comfortable ride, and a sit down. They were the free steamers, the firemans' friend, and if ever a hard word was spoken against them then I never heard it . . . Not once can I remember a bad trip. When my generation of fireman laid hands on them, they were only a few years old, but as they aged, they still retained their passive nature and gentleness. But this gentleness could be deceptive, as when the time came to move the "Grange" it could react with an aggression that belied any thoughts of tranquility. Those small 5ft 8in wheels would start to attack with such power that more than one passenger guard has been left standing on the platform. Then she would up her heels and run, as if the gentle lady had turned into quicksilver.'

R. S. Potts of Tyseley had a very fast run on a 'Grange':[20] 'Bob Templar had done his firing at Old Oak in the 1920s and had a lot of experience and confidence. Both were shown to me once when I was with him on a Saturday evening train from Swindon in 1955. We left there with "Grange" No 6845 *Paviland Grange* with seven coaches, 25 minutes late, with a very easy schedule. Superb confidence gave us very fast running, but No 6845 must have some of the praise as she was in exceptional condition and made the arrival at Snow Hill only one minute late. Unfortunately, it wasn't early enough as Bob was unable to sample a pint because the refreshment room had just closed! A passenger in our train was timing us and told our guard, Joe Kenny, that we were touching 80mph passing Fosse Road [This should have read *90mph* in the published article.] Whether this high speed was accurate or not it is the fastest trip along that fast stretch of line that I have experienced.'

Below:
No 6971 *Athelhampton Hall* takes water from Lapworth troughs on the Birmingham line first opened in 1899. *R. C. Riley*

Left:
No 6990 *Witherslack Hall* rushes past Southall depot with a fitted freight on the evening of 20 June 1961. The round structure behind the water tank in the centre of the picture is a water softening plant. *M. Pope*

Below left:
No 7912 *Little Linford Hall* taking water at Gloucester (Central) with a Bristol-Birmingham express on a dull, rainy day. *G. F. Heiron*

Right:
No 7824 *Iford Manor* taking water at Oxford on 20 July 1963 with the 10.30 Birmingham (Snow Hill) to Eastbourne and Hastings. *B. J. Ashworth*

Below:
No 4705 at Laira Shed (Plymouth) on 25 September 1960. The fuel is a mixture of very large lumps of coal, too big for the firehole, and 'ovoids' – patent fuel officially called Phurnacite. The crane and grab in the background appears to be the method of coaling up some engines. *R. C. Riley*

THE EMISSION OF SMOKE FROM ENGINES MUST BE REDUCED TO THE MINIMUM IN THE OXFORD AREA

GERS MUST OSS THE LINE BY MEANS E SUBWAY

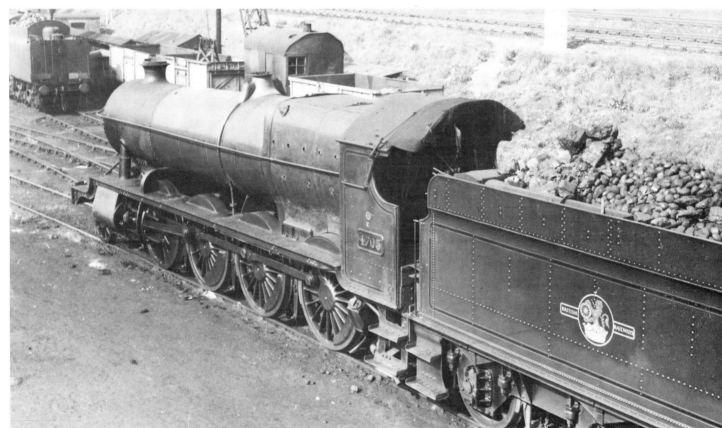

Right:
No 6829 *Burmington Grange*
waiting its turn for coal under the
traditional GW coaling stage at
Newton Abbot on 3 July 1955.
The BR 2-6-2T in front is being
dealt with, note the little narrow
gauge tub which in its turn had
been filled from a standard coal
wagon, all by hand. *R. C. Riley*

Below:
No 7817 *Garsington Manor* at
Chester shed which received a
new roof in 1928 and the hoist
and bucket coaling plant seen
behind the engine. *Real Photos
(R3232)*

Bottom:
No 3955 *Haberfield Hall* in
oil-burning condition at Laira on
22 June 1947. Laira was one of
the GW sheds equipped for oil
refuelling in the abortive postwar
scheme and from where trials
were carried out, some on the
Cornish main line. *R. C. Riley*

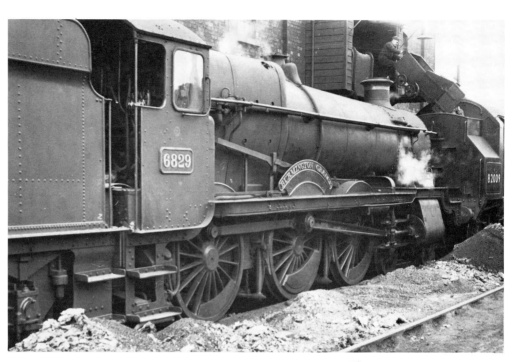

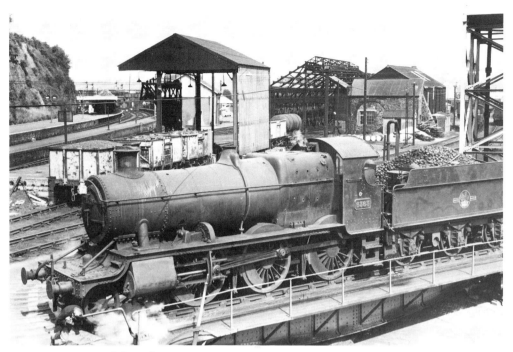

Left:
No 6363 Mogul at Barnstaple
Junction with a tenderful of
'ovoids'. Note the cover at the
whistle connections to the
manifold. *R. C. Riley*

Below:
No 6923 *Croxteth Hall* leaving
Banbury with the 10.08
York-Bournemouth West on 7
March 1964 made up of ex-SR
stock. This is not the best way to
drive and fire (except for
enthusiast run-pasts) and such
slap-dash methods confirmed in
the public mind the steam
locomotive's obsolescence.
G. T. Robinson

Above left:
In contrast No 5939 *Tangley Hall,* seen here at speed with an up goods south of Worcester on 13 April 1960, although being fired is showing almost no smoke; the safety valves are just sizzling too, a sign that the crew are in full command.
R. E. James-Robertson

Left:
Getting ready for some more rain, the fireman of No 6814 *Enborne Grange* is fitting the cab storm sheet. No 6814 is piloting No 6974 *Bryngwyn Hall* at Bath Spa on the 8.20 Bristol (Temple Meads) to Portsmouth Harbour on 17 August 1963. *B. J. Ashworth*

Below left:
Dirty fires and black smoke were not confined to wartime and nationalisation; here No 2921 *Saint Dunstan* leaves a pall of smoke over west London. *Real Photos (51667)*

Top right:
No 6927 *Lilford Hall* at Shipton under Wychwood on 15 May 1964 with a train of coal for Didcot power station, the locomotive utilising 'ovoids'. *T. J. Edgington*

Above right:
Idyllic surroundings on 25 June 1962. No 6993 *Arthog Hall* in spotless condition and decent coal on the tender climbs easily over the Cotswolds towards Sapperton summit with a freight train. With a 'feather' just showing at the safety valve, both enginemen can take in the scenery. *R. C. Riley*

Right:
No 4702 on one of the four turntables in Old Oak Common depot. It was certainly possible to have steam sheds as clean and light as later diesel depots. Eight new sheds were built under Churchward, plus nine straight sheds. Some more sheds were dealt with from 1929 under the Government Loans Act but once World War 2 started, no more time or money was available for steam locomotive running and maintenance improvements or equipment renewal. *Real Photos (W5323)*

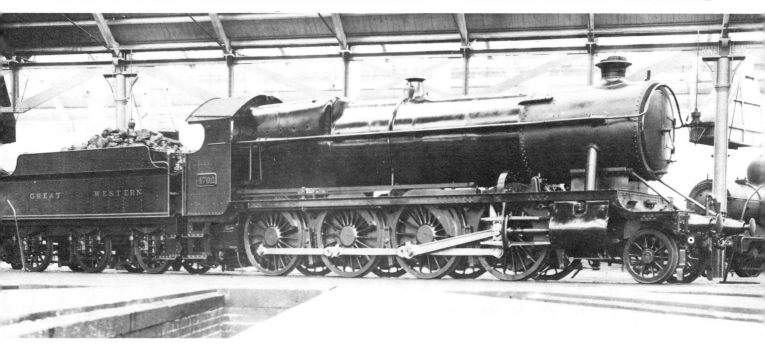

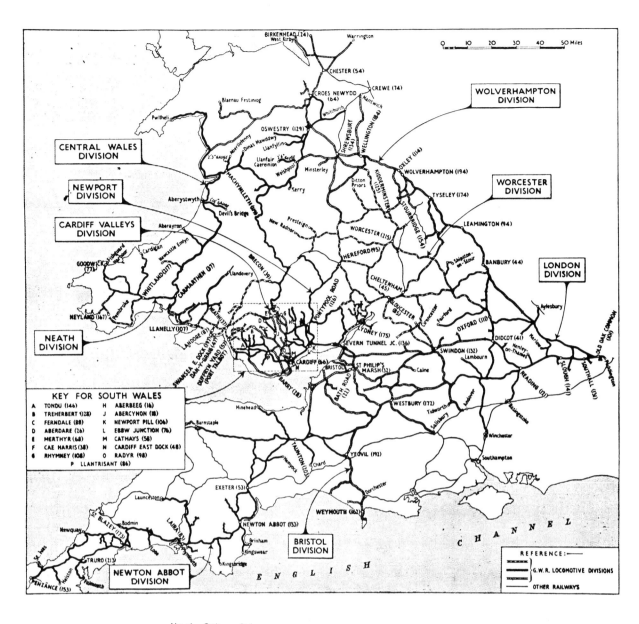

London Division					No. of engines	Code Letter	Code No.
Didcot	...	...	...	...	49	DID	41
Old Oak Common	...	...	...	...	207	PDN	101
Oxford	...	...	...	...	58	OXF	111
Reading	...	...	...	...	102	RDG	121
Southall	...	...	...	...	72	SHL	131
Slough	...	...	...	...	49	SLO	141
Bristol Division							
Bristol (Bath Road)	...	...	...	...	82	BRD	22
Bristol (St. Philip's Marsh)	...	...		...	162	SPM	32
Swindon	...	...	...	...	117	SDN	132
Weymouth	...	...	...	...	25	WEY	162
Westbury	...	...	...	...	69	WES	172
Yeovil	...	...	...	...	9	YEO	192
Newton Abbot Division							
Exeter	...	...	...	...	36	EXE	53
Laira	...	...	...	...	111	LA	83
Newton Abbot	...	...	...	...	70	NA	133
Penzance	...	...	...	...	26	PZ	153
St. Blazey	...	...	...	...	31	SBZ	173
Taunton	...	...	...	...	56	TN	203
Truro	...	...	...	...	21	TR	213
Wolverhampton Division							
Birkenhead	...	...	...	...	38	BHD	24
Banbury	...	...	...	...	77	BAN	44
Chester	...	...	...	...	51	CHR	54
Croes Newydd	...	...	...	...	40	CNYD	64
Crewe	...	...	...	...	2	CRW	74
Leamington	...	...	...	...	26	LMTN	94
Oxley	...	...	...	...	99	OXY	114
Shrewsbury	...	...	...	...	48	SALOP	134
Stourbridge	...	...	...	...	75	STB	154
Tyseley	...	...	...	...	116	TYS	174
Wellington	...	...	...	...	19	WLN	184
Wolverhampton	...	...	...	...	74	SRD	194
Worcester Division							
Cheltenham	...	...	...	...	16	CHEL	45
Gloucester	...	...	...	...	69	GLO	85
Hereford	...	...	...	...	42	HFD	95
Kidderminster	...	...	...	...	19	KDR	125
Lydney	...	...	...	...	22	LYD	175
Worcester	...	...	...	...	98	WOS	215

Newport Division							
Aberbeeg	...	...	...	...	37	ABEEG	16
Aberdare	...	...	...	...	66	ABDR	26
Cardiff	...	...	...	...	133	CDF	66
Ebbw Junction	...	...	...	...	165	NPT	76
Llantrisant	...	...	...	...	21	LTS	86
Newport Pill	...	...	...	...	60	PILL	106
Pontypool Road	...	...	...	...	95	PPRD	126
Severn Tunnel Jc.	...	...	...	...	96	STJ	136
Tondu	...	...	...	...	47	TDU	146
Neath Division							
Carmarthen	...	...	...	...	46	CARM	37
Dan-y-graig	...	...	+	...	38	DG	47
Duffryn Yard	...	...	...	...	63	DYD	57
Goodwick	...	...	...	...	16	FGD	77
Landore	...	...	...	...	59	LDR	87
Llanelly	...	...	...	...	101	LLY	107
Neath	...	...	...	...	66	NEA	137
Neyland	...	...	...	...	23	NEY	167
Swansea East Dock	...	...	...	...	36	SED	197
Whitland	...	...	...	...	22	WTD	217
Cardiff Valleys Division							
Abercynon	...	...	...	...	29	C.V.AYN	18
Barry	...	...	...	...	84	C.V.BRY	28
Cae Harris	...	...	...	...	9	CH	38
Cardiff E. Dock	...	...	...	...	72	CED	48
Cathays	...	...	...	...	57	CHYS	58
Merthyr	...	...	...	...	24	MTHR	68
Ferndale	...	...	...	...	11	C.V.FDL	88
Radyr	...	...	...	...	28	R	98
Rhymney	...	...	...	...	15	RHY	108
Treherbert	...	...	...	...	29	THT	128
Central Wales Division							
Brecon	...	...	...	...	12	BCN	39
Machynlleth	...	...	...	...	51	MCH	119
Oswestry	...	...	...	...	57	OSW	129

Left:
Map showing the Divisional distribution of engine sheds in 1946 *Railway Gazette*

Above:
No 7812 *Erlestoke Manor* **in Dickensian conditions at Wolverhampton Stafford Road in BR days. The only reason there is light available is because most of the roof is missing.** *Ian Allan Library*

Top right:
Such atrocious and dangerous working conditions could dishearten the most eager of workers but some still had a pride in the job. No 5908 *Moreton Hall* **in BR mixed traffic lined black and with red-backed plates is given a final polish at Fishguard on 31 July 1951. The weeds and rubbish are noticeable however.**
R. C. Riley

Right:
No 6800 *Arlington Grange* **sparkling at Penzance shed,** *top* **finishing touches,** *below* **ready for action. The ominous presence of the 'Warship' in the background signals the shape of things to come.** *R. C. Riley*

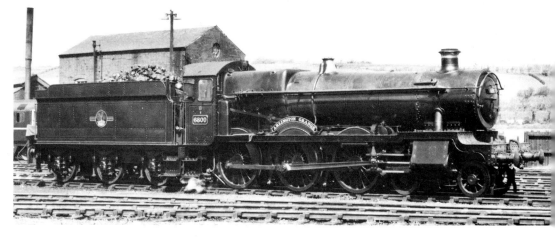

Left:
The conscientious driver of No 6969 *Wraysbury Hall* gives a final top-up to oil boxes whilst waiting to depart from Cardiff (General) with the 1.00pm to Brighton and Portsmouth. *S. Rickard*

Below left:
In order to avoid suffocation, the crew of No 6996 *Blackwell Hall* race down the incline to the Severn Tunnel with the 9.33am Portsmouth-Cardiff on 9 May 1958. *M. Mensing*

Bottom left:
No 6853 *Morehampton Grange* emerges from the claustrophobic depths of Birmingham Snow Hill Tunnel with a down freight on 9 July 1965. *J. H. Cooper-Smith*

Below:
Worcester shed on 13 August 1965 with No 6827 *Llanfrecha Grange* minus name and number plates. No mechanised disposal here! A youth with broom, shovel and wheelbarrow must suffice. *John Hillier*

Top:
No 6873 *Caradoc Grange* at Newton Abbot on 15 July 1961; at this time the shed was being reconstructed as a diesel depot.
R. C. Riley

Above:
Newton Abbot was very busy in the English summertime during the 1950s. Here No 4967 *Shirenewton Hall* of Newton Abbot waits to pilot a 'modified Hall' with a train of LMR stock over the South Devon banks to Plymouth, while other engines await their turn in the shed yard.
R. C. Riley

Left:
Far outpost. No 6301 simmering at Penmaenpool shed on the Barmouth-Ruabon line. The GWR had a considerable number of these small, sub-sheds. *Ian Allan Library*

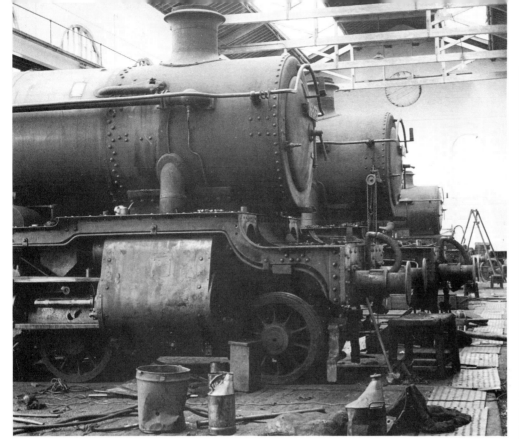

Top left:
Periodic inspection and maintenance was carried out in a number of small workshops attached to the running sheds or in some cases the shed itself. Nos 6873 *Caradoc Grange* and 4920 *Dumbleton Hall* in Worcester Works on 18 April 1964. *T. J. Fairbrother*

Above:
No 1002 *County of Berks* in Oswestry shed. It can be clearly seen that side rods, crossheads and valves can be dealt with without touching the motion, which was only reset (accurately, by machine) on visits to Swindon Works. *E. Kneale*

Above left:
A quartet of GW standard two-cylinder engines headed by No 4937 *Lanelay Hall* were photographed near Denham on 12 August 1951. The other locos consist of one '28xx' and two Moguls. *C. R. L. Coles*

Left:
No 6949 *Haberfield Hall* awaiting repairs, following a mishap. *R. C. Riley*

7
Testing and Performance

For many years the study of locomotive and train running was one of the major branches of the railway hobby and 'logs' of sectional timings of various runs were published (and continue so to be) in the railway enthusiast press. Anthologies of such logs have been published in bookform with linking text and O. S. Nock in particular has published enough data to keep anyone who is interested in Great Western engines, busy for quite some time.[21]

The publishing of official test results, if at all was usually done in professional magazines or learned papers until the days of British Railways when test results for certain locomotive types were made available for public sale in foolscap bookform for a reasonable ten shillings and sixpence each (52½p). Unfortunately there was no consistency between these 'Bulletins' as to presentation of results. No attempt either was made to indicate how reliable any of the results were. In isolation this probably did not matter to any great extent but there was naturally numerous attempts to compare one class with another and obvious discrepancies were assumed to have a basis in original design and were analysed *ad nauseum*. There had always been attempts to calculate horsepowers (usually drawbar horsepower) from stopwatch timings, especially with engines working hard on steep banks with heavy trains. A tendency emerged however, in certain quarters, to mix these calculations with data extracted from test results (some pundits invented their own test results!) and smother with a dressing of rumour and guesswork. The resulting farrago was then presented as a piece of serious research. This obsession with, but inability to properly understand, quantification reached levels worthy of the worst pseudo-scientific excesses of the sociologist and psychologist; this author hopes not to contribute to that quackery. In this chapter will be presented some background to locomotive testing by the Great Western Railway and its successor, illustrated with some typical data from the two-cylinder locomotives, and a few timed logs where certain classes have performed well, out of their normal range. One of the main purposes of testing, the acquisition of consistent performance characteristics on the road, is used in the production of timetable sectional timings (these days by electronic computer), ie the very same thing that the enthusiast has always measured with his stopwatch! Needless to say its not as simple as that, but there can be little doubt that analysis of large numbers of runs with the same locomotive type over the same route and with similar loads can help to build up a fairly accurate picture of a locomotive type's capabilities.

Swindon's advances in testing techniques especially following World War 2 showed a blend of the original with methods advocated elsewhere, but the results were unique and were developed over several decades into a deceptively simple, but in reality very sophisticated system.

Undoubtedly a major influence on the men of Swindon was the Russian, Professor G. V. Lomonossoff. Much of what was learned by Swindon but not understood elsewhere is contained in one of his opening paragraphs to the Institute of Mechanical Engineers in 1931.[22]

'For the average mechanical engineer a locomotive is merely a rolling power plant; whereas in reality it is a means of moving trains, ie an instrument of railway operation. A locomotive not only produces energy but also converts it into the work of propelling a train. It is not only a generator but a consumer of energy. Of course the generation of energy in a locomotive follows the same principles of thermodynamics as in stationary or marine engines, but the laws of its consumption are dictated by the motion of trains. The latter is not in the sphere of thermodynamics, but of railway mechanics. Consequently the knowledge of thermodynamics alone is not sufficient for the rational design and utilization of locomotives. Ignorance of railway mechanics is responsible for the failures of many of the attempts made in the last five years to change radically the form of the locomotive as given by George and Robert Stephenson'.

Some of the earliest testing of all (that bears any resemblance to later work) was performed by that Victorian genius Charles Babbage, in a converted broad gauge passenger brake van in 1839.[23] At this time the broad gauge and Brunel were under attack especially from the *Railway Times* and the directors were getting 'windy'. Babbage's tests were done independently although some of the work on the dynamometer car was financed by Brunel; the 'official expert' was that old gasbag Dr Dionysus Lardner who 'proved' that no train on the wider gauge could travel over 40mph. The decisive meeting of the GW owners was held at the London Tavern on 9 January 1839 when Lardner exhibited his results around the walls. Babbage demolished his every argument and showed his experiments to be meaningless. Babbage's own dynamometer car results had been traced out relentlessly onto large rolls of paper (Babbage had in fact used wallpaper rolls) by pens on his apparatus which had been built by Holtzapffel & Co together with a special clock made by Edward J. Dent & Co. Babbage saved the broad gauge, convincing the northern shareholders of the superiority of Brunel's system. Lardner never forgave Babbage for his utter public humiliation. Gooch took up this experimental spirit with explorations into front-end arrangements and blast-pipe proportions as well as inventing an indicator for use on a moving locomotive in 1847. He also built the first purpose built dynamometer car, known as the 'Measuring Van'. Gooch's early and very thorough test results came at the height of the gauge war and caused some controversy but with hindsight D. K. Clark was to say in 1855:[24]

'Mr Daniel Gooch is the only experimentalist whose results are worthy of implicit confidence, for he operated with the trains precisely under the conditions of ordinary practice.'

Little progress in testing was made in Britain for many years, and although many clever and ingenious instruments were constructed on the Continent they do not seem to have influenced locomotive practice. Most new experimental wisdom came from the laboratories of a number of Alsatian engineers, but this new awareness was concerned purely with the thermodynamics of the steam engine, rather than the mechanics of trains.

The first practical attempts at the proper testing of steam locomotives by the running of a train under controlled conditions were made by Borodin in Russia in the early 1880s.[25] It was Borodin too who made the first steps towards a testing plant, at Kiev around the same time. Tests were conducted on a locomotive held stationary and whose driving wheels acted as belt pulleys; little power could be absorbed but useful results were obtained concerning compounding and the use of steam-jacketed cylinders. The first 'proper' locomotive test plant was built in 1890-1 at Purdue University, Lafayette, Indiana in the USA. It was built by Professor W. F. M. Goss as part of the engineering laboratories for the university, which was under construction. A 40 ton 4-4-0 locomotive was also purchased at the same time. In 1914 when Dean of the College of Engineering at Illinois University Dr Goss, together with Professor E. W. Schmidt (in charge of the department of Railway Enineering) built a very sophisticated plant based on the Pennsylvania Railroad's plant at Altoona. This university also had a half-share in the dynamometer car used on the Illinois Central Railroad. Apart from any direct benefits to locomotive engineering these plants were of immense value as practical educational tools and may well be reflected in the types of locomotive that were built in the later years of steam in the USA which were arguably more relevant than certain European essays, especially to those who conducted the business of running railroads.

In Russia Borodin's road testing ideas were taken up by Lomonssoff who had in Russia available to him, a number of long straight stretches of track, some on constant gradients. It was here that locomotives could be tested at constant output. In order to improve the control of the speed at a constant value a second, assisting (or regulating) locomotive was introduced which helped, to start and accelerate the test train initially and added braking power. In Lomonossoff's time there was developed the 'locomotive passport' which was a booklet of practical characteristics for a given locomotive type and was used by the operating department to rate that type as to its loads and speeds etc. Later, after Lomonossoff had left Russia (the Soviet Union by then) and Stakhanovite endeavour had replaced rational thought, the passports fell into some disrepute. J. N. Westwood has described this all admirably;[26]

'By February 1936 it was clear that work was under way on the recasting of the passports to incorporate the lessons taught by Krivonos [the first Stakhanovite driver]. An article titled *We shall create a new science of traction calculations* pointed out that the existing calculations and passports were based on the work of the "accursed" Lomonosov.'

In Britain it was Churchward who organised the building of the first modern dynamometer car in 1901 while he was assistant to Dean. On becoming Locomotive Superintendent he quickly obtained authorisation for the first (and for very nearly half a century, the only) stationary test plant in Britain.[27] Perhaps his need for the latter was not great as the performance of his new engines was so spectacular, detailed test data was not needed. It spent its first years 'running-in' new locomotives – safer than running them flat out light-engine on the main line. The

dynamometer car was used quite a lot and was lent to other companies, notably the Great Northern Railway.

One of Lomonossoff's pupils, a Pole, Czeczott developed the idea of brake locomotives which could do away with all or part of the train behind the dynamometer car. His method, started in 1921 was taken up by a number of other engineers, notably Nordmann and Günther in Germany, Robson in England (on the LNER) and Chapelon in France. On the continent electric locomotives were occasionally used, utilising regenerative braking, and in Britain this idea was developed in the form of the Mobile Testing Plant on the LMSR. All these methods had one thing in common; they aimed to keep the locomotive under conditions of constant speed (or a series of constant speed steps). Such test trains however could seriously interfere with normal train operations on a busy railway and the resistance of the trailing load was obtained to some extent 'artificially'.

On the GWR, the Controlled Road Testing System was developed which allowed trains to be worked in a normal manner ie speed changing with gradient. The controlled variable on the GW system was the locomotive steam rate (and by implication, the fuel rate) which was kept at a constant value by the driver continually adjusting his cut-off (and therefore speed) in response to any deviation on a special manometer connected to a point below the blast pipe tip which was used as as orifice meter. The road tests were preceded and complemented by tests on Swindon stationary plant which had been modernised in 1936. On the plant a locomotive could be 'tuned' and its thermodynamic characteristics established before being tested with a trailing load on the road.

An important practical factor in the Swindon set-up was that some of the instruments in the dynamometer car were used on the stationary tests too; the car was located adjacent to the locomotive on test, and suitable connections made. The data collected at Swindon, both on the road and the plant was analysed and interpreted by the same team. The complementary nature of these arrangements wasn't unfortunately repeated with the Rugby Testing Station and the Mobile Testing Units. The latter were operated by a completely different team at Derby, and there does seem to have been quite a few difficulties at times in co-ordinating data with regard to certain locomotives tested.

In looking for a scapegoat for these discrepancies Derby turned to – yes, you've guessed it – Swindon! Their steam flow manometer got the blame and Derby invented a fiddle-factor to deal with their own test results and bring them in line with Rugby's. In instructions for the CRT system, Ell had written many years before:[28]

'It must be emphasised that the flow meter is used only as an indicator *Not* for the actual determination of the steam rate. Whether the actual rate obtained is the same as that estimated for is unimportant provided the steam and coal rates are constant and are properly measured by the Summation of Increment Method.' and later, 'If the plots for the water injected can be fairly represented by a straight line then the slope of this line establishes the water-rate; similarly the slope of the coal line establishes the coal rate. *If either cannot be so represented, the test is rejected.*'

'This metering [of feed water] is done by special apparatus in the dynamometer car and transferred to the fireman in the form of high or low water level lights to which he works for the control of the injectors.'

Unlike the Derby system, that at Swindon was self-checking, a speed curve was plotted for a test along a route from other test data (ie plant) and actual speeds then plotted as the train ran at a predetermined steam rate. These results usually agreed to a remarkable extent; no such confirmation was possible by the Derby methods and their case against Swindon does not stand up but rather implies inadequate experimental techniques on their own part.

The Controlled Road Testing System was also used for the Gas Turbines and also various main line diesel classes; a new sophisticated dynamometer car being introduced in 1961, converted from a Hawksworth third class coach built in 1946. This contained a number of X-Y plotters which could automatically plot drawbar characteristics etc. Interestingly the very last (for the time being!) steam locomotive tests in Britain were carried out with this vehicle in 1963 when an 'Austerity' 0-6-0ST owned by the National Coal Board and fitted with a Hunslet underfed stoker, gas-producer firebox and 'Kylpor' blast arrangement was given thorough testing on the OWW line of the Western Region.

With a constant steam rate (or fuel rate in a diesel) the actual drawbar pull/train speed relationship is uniquely defined irrespective of gradient. The tractive force applied at the locomotive driving wheels to the whole train is a large percentage of the force produced in the cylinders and like the latter is not affected by gradient. The drawbar pull on the trailing load is in proportion to the tractive force applied to the whole train, in the ratio of the trailing mass to the gross train mass. The system has the advantage that it is operating under the second law of motion which is the general equation for the motion of a train, whereas constant speed testing with brake units operates under the third law.

Of the fundamental measurements taken in a road test those of train and locomotive resistance are most important. Figures for the former (modern passenger stock) measured on the Western Region were corroborated in test after test and can be taken as exceptionally reliable.

Locomotive resistance is a very thorny problem as it is very difficult to measure. For example if a locomotive is working very hard and producing say 2,000hp in the cylinders and 1,500hp at the drawbar with say a tolerance of ±3% the figures would be quite acceptable to engineers or timetable compilers but the difference (ie the locmotive resistance) will not be 500hp ±3% but could be anything between 375hp and 605hp, the second figure being 61% greater than the first. Unless the resistance of a locomotive has been measured by testing and presented by use of a good clear graph with stated wind allowances etc, its numerical expression is usually very misleading and often meaningless 'data for the sake of data'.

At Swindon the thermodynamic testing was done on the stationary plant and indicated characteristics developed; these were confirmed and the corresponding drawbar characteristics obtained on the road with the dynamometer car. However, in presenting the data for practical use by railwaymen and for compiling schedules and timetables the drawbar characteristics were shown for 'average wind conditions' usually a 7½mph, 45° headwind. Ell explained in his paper to the Institute of Locomotive Engineers.[29]

'Here a wide scatter is observable due to the varying wind effect on the locomotive, as during the test series, the natural wind velocity varied between 7mph against and in favour of the train. The speed lines are therefore *given a bias towards the adverse conditions* [Authors's italics] which are considered to be applicable to the drawbar characteristics that are ultimately produced from them. The differences between the indicated and equivalent drawbar efforts are, of course the engine resistances.'

This of course means that the engine resistances are also biased on the high side and should not therefore be compared willy-nilly with those obtained elsewhere as has so often been done especially when those elsewhere often appear implausibly low.

It is of course possible to treat locomotive resistance from a theoretical and analytical point of view, and for those interested, the following is the formula used by, among others, André Chapelon following World War 2:

$$R = \Sigma \ (0.02 \tfrac{d}{D})P_s + E_i \ (0.06 + \tfrac{r_c}{100}) + 4.5 \tfrac{100}{V^2}$$

where:

d	= journal diameter	V	= speed (km/hr)
D	= wheel diameter	r_c	= $0.9n^2 - 4n + 6.5$
P_s	= load on journal (kg)		
E_i	= indicated te (kg)	n	= speed (revs/sec)

It is not a straightforward matter to show the superiority of Churchward's locomotives over others as very little data has survived and other than one or two exacting express schedules the work they did was well within their capacity. Indeed there was little in the whole steam age in Britain to overtax the 'Saints' (or 'Stars') other than a few very heavy long distance expresses on the Northern lines. No 171 *Albion* undoubtedly showed a great deal of superiority over No 102 *La France* as it was itself an improvement over No 100 and No 98, the latter which was shown capable of greater power output than *La France*. All three of these first 4-6-0s showed marked less fuel consumption for exactly the same trains, over a period of months. Oil consumption on the compound was 8-9lb/100 miles as against 4-6lb/100 miles for *Albion*. In various talks given to Swindon Junior Engineering Society concerned with compound locomotives, the opinion was put forward that it was the superiority of the GW boiler that 'masked' the efficiency of the French compounds when comparisons were made. Churchward bought another two of the continental machines, of a larger size and fitted one with a Swindon No 1 boiler after it had been in service a couple of years. At 33.4sq ft the grates on these engines as built were almost as big as a 'King' and the heating surface of 2,757sq ft was 29% greater than *Albion*. When starting as simples the tractive effort was about 45,500lb or nearly twice as much as *Albion* (23,090lb). This made them very susceptible to excessively violent slipping if attempts were made to accelerate heavy trains too quickly. Continual slipping was noted too on the south Devon banks.[30] The obvious benefits of divided drive were taken up by Chruchward, better balance and smooth running at speed, but he was not convinced by compounding. It has been suggested that had he bought one of the Nord '3500' class 4-6-0s with 5ft 9in coupled wheels, introduced in 1908, he might have changed his mind.

There is though, no evidence whatever that these engines were particularly good until considerably rebuilt and 'tuned' in the 1930s. Figures produced at that time show that before rebuilding, but when superheated the *maximum* output was 1,370dbhp at 70km/hr. (43.5mph). In their saturated form they certainly seem on reflection to have been sluggish at speed although their fans at the time saw everything through rosé tinted glasses. Lord Monkswell wrote:

'Some of the express trains on the Nord which stop frequently, are worked by six-coupled engines with wheels 5ft 9in in diameter. That these engines are by no means unable to run fast was made apparent by one of them – No 3.515 – with a load of 305 tons, attaining a speed of 73.6mph down the bank of 1 in 200 between Survilliers and Paris. But as was to be expected, though the engine was in first-rate order and ran with great smoothness, she did not reach this speed so easily as the 4-4-2 engines with bigger driving wheels.'

One would have thought that almost *any* locomotive would reach that sort of speed *down* the fourteen or so miles of Survilliers bank, with 305 tons of train pushing it, with great assistance from gravity. The GW 5ft 8in 'Granges' are known to have topped 90mph and a log will be included in this chapter where one ran the 13.4 miles from Uffington to Didcot at an average of 71 mph with 485 tons gross. This with an engine 100% Churchward in concept and on almost level track. The mythology of pre-World War 1 continental compounds reflects a romanticism introduced by such writers as Walter Scott and Bulwer Lytton, even if it was dubious history. Winston Churchill summed up this attitude. 'If episodes like this did not happen, they *ought* to have happened'.

The test data included has of necessity to be brief, a dynamometer can run with *Albion* is included and so are some characteristics for 'Saint' class 4-6-0s taken from a test run. Curves of this nature were marked up for all engine classes in a book kept with considerable security in Swindon drawing office (but where is it now?). This was of course long before the days of S. O. Ell and company. A summary of tests on the stationary plant of Hawksworths first 'County' 4-6-0 No 1000 was recently found but the original data seems not to have survived, however the summary is included here and shows the class to be thermally better than supposed 'more modern' engines – ie BR 'Britannia'. The 'County' has a lesser specific steam consumption in spite of a lower superheat, for this speed and steam rate.

Drawing Office,
Swindon
25 August 1945

Engine No 1000 on Testing Plant

Results of Steam Consumption tests on Thursday and Friday 23 and 24 August 1945 from a preliminary examination of records, and are subject to later confirmation.

Conditions of Test:
Duration 1 hour; 20% cut-off; full regulator speed 45mph; Markham coal.

Observations, Indicator Cards etc:
Boiler Pressure, Quantities of Water and Coal used, Smokebox and Ashpan Vacuum, Temperatures of Steam entering and leaving cylinders and in base of Blast Pipe; Temperatures of Smokebox Gases leaving Superheater and Small Flues; Smokebox Gas and Coal analyses.
Indicator Cards from Cylinder (one with weak spring to enlarge the exhaust line) and Steam Chest.
Pressure at base of Blast Pipe by Mercury Manometer.
Time and Revolutions recorded electrically.

Results:
Water per hour from 63°F to steam superheated 170°F
(temperature 584°F) 18,220lb
Coal per hour 2,688lb
Firing rate per hour .... 93lb/sq ft grate
Water/lb coal 6.8
Mean effective Pressure .... 82lb/sq in
ihp 1,342
ihp per sq ft grate 46.5
Steam per ihp/hour 13.6lb

Coal per ihp/hour 2.0lb
Pressure at base of blast pipe .... 2.4lb/sq in
Smokebox Vacuum .... 5.5in water

The above were obtained from the first test; they were confirmed by the second test.

General:
The boiler with the double blast pipe steamed extremely well and at no time was the fireman in difficulties either in the first test when the fire and smokebox both were clean, or in the second when the fire was dirty and the smokebox filled with ash reaching almost to the tip of the forward blast pipe in the front, though the bottom row of small flues were never blocked.

Following nationalisation one of the 'Modified Halls' was given thorough workouts on the testing plant and also with the dynamometer car on the road. It was at this time that the benefits of the exhaust steam injector were quantified.

A 'Manor' was tested in 1951 and was the first GWR type to be dramatically 'tuned up'; an earlier patient having been the LMS Ivatt Class 2, 2-6-0. The 'Manors' had been usually seen on secondary lines, especially on the lines in central Wales. Their ejector was rather small limiting their brake power and they had no exhaust steam injector. While probably better than a 'Dukedog' they weren't regarded as good steamers, especially by main line crews. The boilers were based on the same ratios as other GW types as was the draughting, and this was the rub. The draughting could not be just scaled down on an *ad hoc* basis. In the event a slightly smaller blast pipe tip, a longer thinner chimney with smaller choke and a little increase in the free grate area transformed the boiler and its output went up by 120%, to approximately 1,000lb/sq ft of grate per hour. There is no doubt that this episode showed that there was nothing magical about locomotive performance and that correctly proportioned draughting was essential and could be obtained without resort to complicated, patented, foreign gadgets. Later most of the larger engines were investigated on the plant, the 'Kings', 'Counties' and some 'Castles' receiving double blast pipes and chimneys.

In 1952, in accordance with a Minute from the Locomotive Testing Committee a train timing exercise was carried out to ascertain if any overall coal consumption could accrue from variations in loads and speeds. Tests were carried out on three regions. The Western Region used No 6988 *Swithland Hall* which was in fair condition and in accordance with the description of the engine tested and described in Bulletin No 1. Blidworth Cobbles, Grade 2B, was used throughout the tests (this wasn't normally available at Swindon so they borrowed from the Test Plant supply.) The coal consumption measurement on these tests was carried out using a self weighing tender. This enabled the amounts used for the following to be ascertained: lighting up; light engine movements, cleaning fires and general wastage; whilst running trains. Locomotive running performance and analysis were obtained from a small recorder which was carried in the vehicle next to the tender. To that, time in half minutes, location by milepost, and engine working were transmitted electrically. The information on the records enabled large scale speed-distance-time diagrams to be prepared from which the running and coal consumption analyses were made.
The observed turns were as follows:

Passenger services; the rostered turn consisted of:
a) 9.00am Swindon to Paddington passenger, usual load 11

coaches of about 346 tons tare, calling at Challow, Didcot and Reading.

b) 1.18pm Paddington to Weston-super-Mare, usual load 11 coaches of about 346 tons tare to Swindon, but increased to 13 coaches of about 403 tons on days observed, nine of about 279 tons tare from Swindon to Bristol, and 4 of about 124 tons tare from Bristol to Weston. The train calls at Reading, Didcot, Wantage Road, Challow, Swindon, Chippenham, Bath, Bristol and intermediate stations to Weston.

c) 8.25pm. Weston-super-Mare to Swindon calling at all stations.

Only parts a) and b) were kept under observation. From the results some interesting points emerged. For a recovery of five minutes by the locomotive due to out of course delays increases the coal consumption on the basic by 21.3%. Test plant results showed that had Welsh coal been used (Markham), the higher quality, in spite of being 19% saved in quantity and 5½ on price.

Fast freight services; the rostered turn selected for observation consisted of:

a) 3.35pm Swindon to Banbury fish empties, booked to stop at Oxford, and at Oxford North Yard, if required, to pick up load.

b) 7.30pm. Banbury to Swindon fish booked to stop at Oxford and Marston Sidings to drip load.

The round trip of 112 miles was kept under observation on two consecutive days.

Normal Freight Services; the rostered turn selected for observation consisted of the 1.20pm Swindon to Weymouth freight stopping at Chippenham, Trowbridge, Westbury, Castle Cary, Yeovil, Maiden Newton and Dorchester for picking up and/or dropping load. The trip of 91 miles was kept under observation on two days.

It was found that on passenger services, a 4% allowance of extra coal was needed above that obtained from test bulletins; this for lighting up, wastage etc. This was 5.4% for fast freight service and 15% for ordinary freight service. It was thought the latter was due to low values of specific resistance for freight trains, being used in the computation of the consumption under power.

Over the next few years Swindon developed their 'Technical Train Timing' ably described by S. O. Ell in his paper *The Mechanics of the Train in the Service of Railway Operation* read to the Institution of Locomotive Engineers in 1958.

Some Notable Runs
In 1923 the afternoon 'Cheltenham Spa Express' was speeded up from Swindon to Paddington requiring 75 minutes for the 77.3 miles; an average speed of almost 62mph start to stop. On the first trip 'Saint' No 2915 *Saint Bartholomew* handled the job with consummate ease. Cecil J. Allen, who was on the train wrote:[31]

'. . . the moment we were away from Swindon all my doubts were set at rest – that is, short of a breakdown or some other fearsome casualty. [He had a tight connection to make.] The acceleration out of Swindon was perfectly amazing. At the end of 2¾ miles we were doing 61½mph; at 3¼, 65mph; at 3¾, 69mph; at 4¼, 72½mph; and at 4¾, 74mph – that is to say we were up to 74mph in less than five miles from the dead start, and on the level! . . . we positively ambled into Paddington, getting a perfectly clear road, and arrival 1min 25sec before time, despite the afore-mentioned amble, and two delays costing at least 4min between them! Under 70min net for a journey of 77.3 miles, and a slow finish to avoid too early an arrival! If the Great Western is

setting out seriously to capture and retain the blue riband of start-to-stop railway speed, as I remarked previously, in such circumstances as these it would seem idle for any other aspirant so much as to attempt to compete!'

Most of the later 'Saints' and some earlier ones had 'Hall' pattern cylinders on renewal, and outside steam pipes. Although there were good reasons for this, the engines weren't as free running as those with the original Churchward cylinders with vast internal steam passages. ('Granges' and 'Manors' however had greatly increased steam chest volumes in their cylinder patterns.) The 'Saints' were long lived and well loved engines capable of anything, yet simple and robust but deceptively powerful and efficient.

In emergencies mixed traffic engines were sometimes appropriated for use on the hardest express duties. That they could take on these tasks is well illustrated by the exploits of 2-6-0 No 8326 in 1933 with 14 coaches of 465 tons gross on the second part of the 6.10 ex-Paddington. It took this load over hill and down dale; 57.2 miles to Ardley in 66min 50sec at a speed of 51.35mph. An average output of nearly 1,200ihp would be required for this and nearer 1,500ihp for some of the harder parts intermittently. This was a remarkable performance from this small boiler (the same as the 'City' 4-4-0s) and showed enginemanship at its absolute finest.[32]

I have included here a couple of logs on the old GW main line. One is the famous run of No 7904 *Fountains Hall* on the up 'Britolian' of 15 September 1954 following the removal of a 'Castle', due to dragging brakes, at Little Somerfod, the second is No 6832 *Brockton Grange* which replaced a failed 'Britannia' Pacific at Swindon on a Cardiff to Paddington express. Finally I have included a run of a 'Manor' from Wolverhampton to Wellington. This little engine reached 81mph down the descent to Cosford and climbed the bank from Shifnal to Hollinswood with a minimum speed of 50mph.

WR: Swindon-Paddington
Engine: 4-6-0 No 6832 *Brockton Grange*
Load 14 coaches, 445 tons tare, 485 tons gross

Dist		Actual		Speeds
		min	sec	mph
0.0	SWINDON	0	00	–
3.5	*Marston East*	–		–
5.7	Shrivenham	9	32	58
10.8	Uffington	14	24	67½
–				
13.4	Challow	16	43	70
16.9	Wantage Road	19	39	72
20.8	Steventon	22	53	73
24.2	DIDCOT	25	40	74
28.8	Cholsey	29	37	70
–		p.w.s.		40
35.8	Pangbourne	37	39	62
38.6	Tilehurst	40	14	64½
41.3	READING	42	52	63
46.3	Twyford	47	45	60
53.1	Maidenhead	sig.		65
		stop		0
56.3	Burnham	60	47	54½
58.8	SLOUGH	62	23	61
–		–		–
64.1	West Drayton	68	43	57
68.2	Southall	72	53	58
71.6	Ealing	76	23	62
–		–		–
76.0	Westbourne Park	81	24	–
77.3	PADDINGTON	84	14	–
	Depart from Swindon		85 late	
	Net time: min		80	

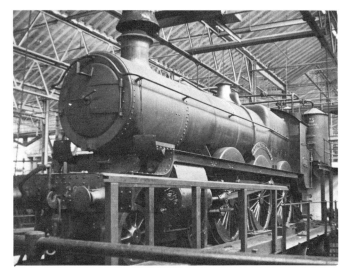

WR: Little Somerford-Paddington

Engine: 4-6-0 No 7904, *Fountains Hall*
Load: 7 coaches, 230 tons tare, 245 tons gross

Dist		Sched	Actual		Speeds
Miles		min	sec		mph
0.0	LITTLE SOMERFORD	†0	0	00	–
2.7	Brinkworth	–	3	45	65
6.8	Wootton Bassett	8	7	39	66
12.4	SWINDON	13	12	33	79
18.1	Shrivenham	–	17	05	76
23.2	Uffington	*	20	56	77
25.8	Challow	–	23	02	78
29.3	Wantage Road	–	25	45	80
33.2	Steventon	31½	28	43	80
36.6	DIDCOT	33½	31	14	82
41.2	Cholsey	–	34	37	82
45.0	Goring	–	37	19	80
48.2	Pangbourne	–	39	41	82/84
53.7	READING	45½	43	41	83
58.7	Twyford	49	47	18	80/83
65.5	Maidenhead	54	52	10	83
71.2	SLOUGH	58½	56	25	82
76.5	West Drayton	–	60	22	80
80.6	SOUTHALL	65	63	35	75
84.0	Ealing Broadway	*	66	15	73
88.4	Westbourne Park	75	70	01	–
89.7	PADDINGTON	79	72	10	–

*Includes 4 min recovery margin. †Assumed

WR: Wolverhampton-Wellington

Engine: 4-6-0 No 7822, *Foxcote Manor*
Load: 6 coaches, 192 tons tare, 205 tons gross

Dist		Times		Speeds
Miles		min	sec	mph
0.0	WOLVERHAMPTON	0	00	–
2.3	Oxley North Junc	4	45	60
4.8	Codsall	7	15	52/60/56
7.8	Albrighton	10	14	72
9.1	Cosford Halt	11	20	81
12.5	Shifnal	14	08	68
14.5	Madeley Junc	16	12	52
15.4	Hollinswood	17	25	50
16.6	Oakengates	18	30	72
17.7	New Hadley Halt	19	27	75
19.6	WELLINGTON	21	45	–

Top:
No 2931 Arlington Court on the Plant in June 1935. *Real Photos (18337)*

Above:
No 4930 Hagley Hall with the dynamometer car and indicator shelter for road testing in GW days. (c.1931). *Real Photos (W2351)*

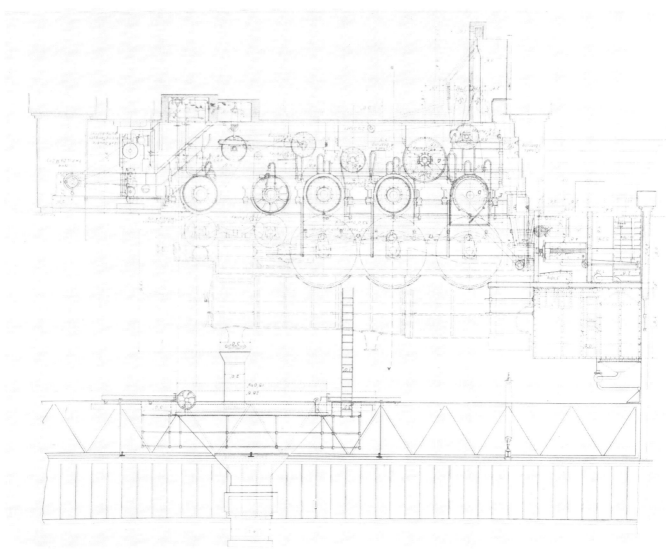

Above:
Churchward's original Test Plant set-up. First schemed in the late 1890s as part of the works facilities *four* plants were envisaged to keep the factory supplied with compressed air whilst running-in new locomotives. *Author's collection*

Left:
The locomotive exchanges: In 1948 the nationalised British Railways ran a series of interchange trials. GWR No 6990 *Witherslack Hall* was used on the Great Central line. No 6990 on a down Manchester express passing through Arkwright Street, Nottingham on 24 June 1948. *J. P. Wilson*

Right:
Two days earlier, on the same train No 6990 passes Bagthorpe Junction in a rainstorm. *J. P. Wilson*

Above:
Two Swindon stalwarts with rebuilt Bulleid 'Merchant Navy' pacific No 35020 *Bibby Line,* on test in June 1956 with the Swindon dynamometer car on the Waterloo-Exeter line of the ex-LSWR. Second from the left and acting footplate observer on that occasion is the late Ernie Nutty (note the telephone equipment for communication with the dynamometer car). Fourth from the left is the incomparable S.O. ('Sammy') Ell, one of the greatest of the behind-the-scenes locomotive engineers and a great innovator in experimental method. *Crown Copyright/NRM*

Top right:
The 'Manors' were the first of the two-cylinder classes to have modifications to their draughting. No 7818 *Granville Manor* was the guinea-pig and is seen here with a very thin chimney.
T. E. Williams/NRM

Above right:
The pioneer 'County' had been built with a double chimney and was given full road tests in 1954. Here *County of Middlesex* shunts its train at Stoke Gifford Yard during tests on 19 January 1954.
Ivo Peters

Right:
Outside Swindon Works after tests and modifications to the blastpipes. *G. Wheeler*

Above:
No 1009 *County of Carmarthen* in the same position in October 1954 and fitted with S. O. Ell's modified draughting to take account of increased superheat plus the addition of self-cleaning plates (later replaced by a basket-type spark-arrestor). This double chimney arrangement was later used successfully on the 'Kings' and some 'Castles' as well as a number of '9Fs' (but *not* No 71000 whose blast arrangement was designed by Derby DO). *G. Wheeler*

Right:
Running through Swindon on one of the tests. *R. C. H. Nash*

Below:
No 6955 *Lydcott Hall* on 10 March 1958 at Swindon during brake tests. *G. Wheeler*

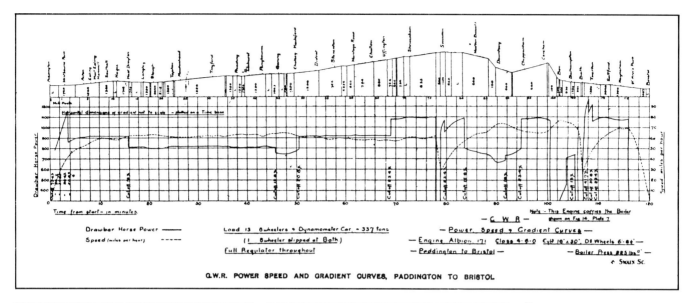

Q.W.R. POWER SPEED AND GRADIENT CURVES, PADDINGTON TO BRISTOL

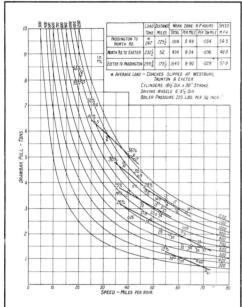

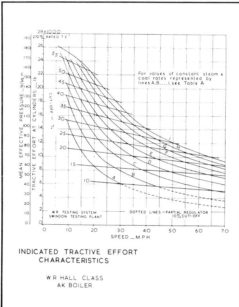

INDICATED TRACTIVE EFFORT CHARACTERISTICS

W R HALL CLASS
AK BOILER

Above:
Summary of a Dynamometer Car run with 4-6-0 No 171 *Albion* **on 13 April 1904.** *The Engineer*

Far left:
Characteristic curve for a 'Saint'. This was the standard method of presenting a locomotive type's capabilities for many years on the GWR until the more sophisticated Controlled Road Testing methods were developed. *Railway Gazette*

Left:
Indicated tractive effort for the 'Modified Hall' as derived from the stationary plant.

Below left: **The tables of values for any given steam rate shows dramatically the differences that are obtained from coal variations and the enormous benefits of the exhaust steam injector at all rates of working but especially at the higher ones.** *British Railways*

LINE	MARKHAM (SOUTH WALES) GRADE 1 COAL G.C.V. AS FIRED 14330 B.Th.U./lb									BLIDWORTH HARD GRADE 2 COAL G.C.V. AS FIRED 12500 B.Th.U./lb									
	LIVE STEAM INJECTOR				EXHAUST STEAM INJECTOR					LIVE STEAM INJECTOR				EXHAUST STEAM INJECTOR				
	STEAM		COAL		STEAM		FEED WATER	HEAT ABOVE FEED	COAL		STEAM		HEAT ABOVE FEED	COAL		STEAM		FEED WATER	HEAT ABOVE	COAL	
	lb/hr	Temp °F	lb/hr	lb/sq ft grate/hr	lb/hr	Temp °F	lb/hr	B.Th.U./lb	lb/hr	lb/sq ft grate/hr	lb/hr	Temp °F	B.Th.U./lb	lb/hr	lb/sq ft grate/hr	lb/hr	Temp °F	lb/hr	B.Th.U./lb	lb/hr	lb/sq ft grate/hr
A	8000	523	1266	825	30.5	8140	490	7570	1239	20	26.6	8090	500	1244	925	34.2	8090	500	7530	1244	850	31.4
B	10000	542	1269	1060	39.2	10120	521	9420	1255	940	34.7	10080	528	1258	1205	44.5	10080	528	9310	1258	1110	41.0
C	12000	555	1275	1320	48.7	12110	543	11270	1266	1150	42.5	12070	547	1268	1525	56.3	12070	547	11220	1268	1390	51.3
D	14000	564	1280	1615	59.6	14090	557	13110	1273	1390	51.3	14060	561	1275	1880	69.4	14060	561	13080	1275	1710	63.1
E	16000	571	1283	1945	71.8	16070	568	14950	1278	1660	61.3	16060	569	1279	2295	84.7	16060	569	14930	1279	2070	76.4
F	18000	576	1286	2325	85.8	18060	575	16800	1282	1950	72.0	18060	577	1283	2840	104.8	18060	577	16800	1283	2500	92.3
G	20000	580	1288	2840	104.8	20050	580	18650	1285	2290	84.6	20050	585	1287	3815	141.0	20050	585	18650	1287	3075	113.6
H	22000	584	1290	3780	139.7	22040	586	20500	1288	2690	99.4											
I	24000					24040	590	22360	1290													

FRONT END LIMITS

| 21500 | 583 | 1289 | 3400 | 125.7 | 23110 | 589 | 21500 | 1289 | 2972 | 109.8 |

ABOVE GRATE LIMIT

GRATE LIMITS

| 22200 | 584 | 1290 | 4180 | 154.3 | 25590 | 593 | 23800 | 1292 | 4345 | 160.3 | 20200 | 590 | 1290 | 4260 | 157.2 | 21690 | 588 | 20200 | 1289 | 4260 | 157.2 |

To adjust firing rate for other coals of known gross calorific value

Soft Coals
Multiply firing rate values in the appropriate Markham column by 14330 and divide by the G.C.V. of the coal. For these coals, capacity is limited by draught requirements and maximum firing rates for any soft coal must not exceed those given in "Front End Limit" columns for Markham coal.

Hard Coals
Multiply firing rate values in the appropriate Blidworth column by 12500 and divide by the G.C.V. of the coal. For these coals, capacity is limited by grate capacity only and maximum firing rates for any hard coal must not exceed those given in "Grate Limit" columns for Blidworth coal.

W R TESTING SYSTEM
SWINDON TESTING PLANT

W R HALL CLASS
AK BOILER

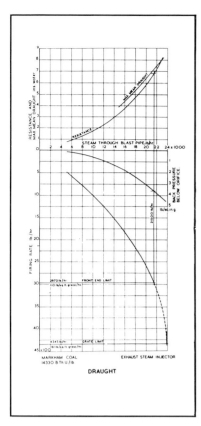

Above:
Boiler efficiency and Equivalent Evaporation characteristics for both Markham and Blidworth coals. *British Railways*

Right:
Front end characteristics for 'improved draughting'. Swindon used the blast nozzle as a limiting device – a limit to be reached before the grate limit was reached in order to prevent unnecessary and wasteful thrashing of engines. *British Railways*

Below right:
A Controlled Road Test Summary for the 'Modified Hall'. *British Railways*

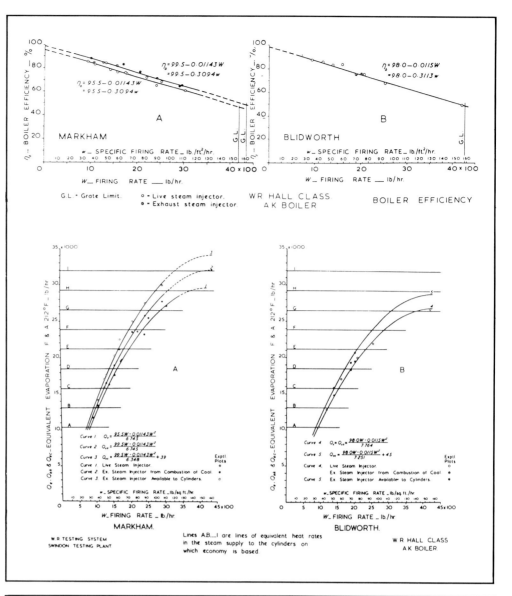

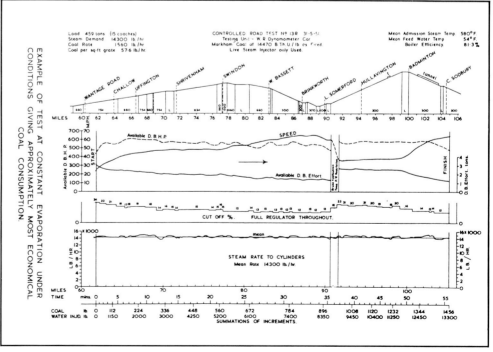

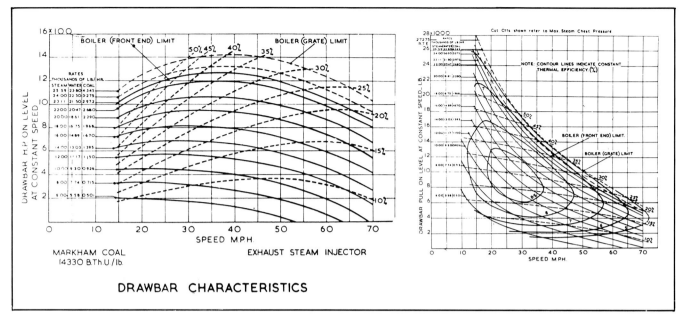

DRAWBAR CHARACTERISTICS

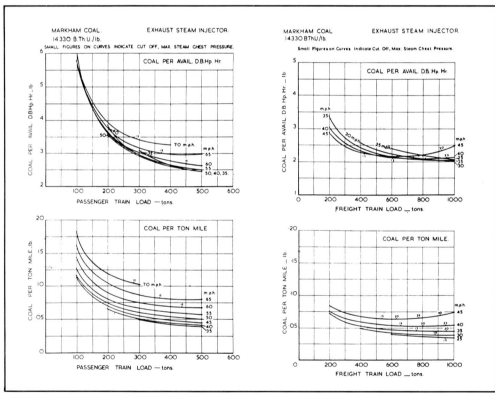

Above:
Drawbar horsepower characteristics as ascertained from CRT with cut-off/steam rate/speed data from stationary plant tests. *British Railways*

Left:
Passenger and Freight train coal consumption curves for different loads and speeds *on the level* – several sets of curves were prepared for different gradients. *British Railways*

8
Modifications

The first major modification made by the GW following the introduction of the 'Halls' was in fact carried out on a 20 year old 'Saint', No 2935 *Caynham Court* which in May 1931 was rebuilt with Rotary Cam Poppet valve gear and new cylinders. This increased the weight by three tons; the blastpipe was increased to 5⅜in diameter.

Tests showed an increase in coal consumption per DBHP of 44% as against a standard 'Saint' (5.14lb as against 3.57lb, per DBHP) and that with a higher calorific value of coal. Over 22% less water was evaporated per pound of coal, due to the lowering of boiler efficiency. These results were reflected in the opening paragraphs of a paper read by S. O. Ell to the (GWR) Swindon Engineering Society in 1933:[33]

'The cylinder problem of the locomotive is entirely different from that of the stationary engine. With the latter, the size of the cylinder and the steam distribution has to be determined for economical working with a given load at a given speed; with the former, the cylinder is made of a size which will start the heaviest train permitted by the adhesion of the locomotive. This cylinder must then be used to the best advantage at a greatly increased speed but under a greatly reduced mean effective pressure.

'Failure to realise this important difference caused that catenation of severe criticism which was levelled at the locomotive valve gear. Indeed no outstanding, successful, mechanical device has ever been so consistently assailed. The distribution which it gives is so unlike what is considered good in stationary engine practice, and so like what is considered bad in that practice, that many regarded it almost with contempt as a device whose only virtue was that it kept going. But an opportunity to justify these criticisms was afforded on the introduction of the poppet-valve gear, in which the desired steam distribution can be effected by cams having suitable profiles.

'The advocates of this type of gear reasoned that, by thus providing a quicker opening of the valve on admission and a very rapid closing of the valve at cut off, practical prevention of wiredrawing would be accomplished and more work obtained from each pound of steam used. Further, by making the compression periods shorter, it would be possible to work the engine in an earlier, and they argued, a more economical cut off.

'Practical prevention of wiredrawing certainly is accomplished as indicator diagrams clearly show. But these diagrams also show that the expansion line falls more rapidly than is usual with long travel piston valve-linkage gear operation. The net result is that, although superheated steam is used, the mean effective pressure is lower, and the fuel economy expected to follow the displacement of the piston valve does not materialise.

'The undue pressure drop during expansion is probably caused somewhat by exhaust valve leakage and, chiefly, by greater cylinder condensation.

'With regard to the first, the exhaust valves and passages,

having been cooled by the exhaust steam, condense some live steam. It is known that the viscosity of water at any particular temperature is much less than that of steam at the same temperature, so that, although a valve may be perfectly steam tight it is not necessarily water tight as well and some heat is lost by condensate passing through the valves. Indeed Professor Callendar believed that the greater part of the steam which cannot be accounted for in the indicator diagram is lost in this way. If, therefore, there is reason to believe that poppet valves are not as steam tight as piston valves it is not difficult to realise that more heat is lost by the greater quantity of condensate which the exhaust poppet valves will pass.

'With regard to the second, if the steam temperature cycle and metal temperature cycle, established from tests by Callendar and Nicolson, be compared, it will be found that the metal cycle does not even approximately follow the steam cycle. From a pronounced level during admission, the steam temperature, immediately after cut off, falls away on a very definite incline. In the metal cycle, the temperature rises and falls with equal gradients, reaching a maximum value after 30% of the stroke has been traversed by the piston. At the usual running cut offs the metal temperature is therefore still rising after cut off has taken place. The metal must absorb this heat from the steam, now, improvidently, falling in pressure and temperature. Consequently, there is a great tendency towards condensation at this period.

'Something evidently occurs in the linkage gear operation to counteract it which does not obtain in cam operation. In an example of the former, in 25% cut off and with a lead of ³⁄₁₆in the maximum port opening to steam is 0.36in. When the piston has moved 4⅝in from the commencement of its stroke the valve, closing, gives a port opening just ³⁄₁₆in again. Whilst moving this amount to cut off the piston moves 2⅜in, equivalent to a crank angle of 12°, illustrating, in the linkage gear the somewhat gradual closing of the valve to steam. Wiredrawing to some extent, therefore, occurs, expansion probably commences before mechanical cut off, and the throttling action on the steam provides some degree of additional superheat to help counteract the condensation tendency at the very time it is needed.

'It must not be thought, however, that matters would be improved still further by any increase in this throttling action – any such attempt would prove otherwise. Nevertheless, in the author's opinion, it is established that what does take place with long travel valves is, far from being harmful, a very definite advantage. Matters would only be improved for cam operation if a very high superheat were used. The advisability of this is very much doubted. A very high superheat in a locomotive means robbing an already limited boiler of heat which would otherwise be used for evaporation, higher maintenance costs in the superheater itself, and lubrication difficulties in the cylinders where increased maintenance costs would undoubtedly ensue.

'With regard to reducing the compression and earlier working by cam gear, if the compression period be made shorter than that provided by good piston valve-linkage gear operation, sufficient steam is not trapped for cushioning the reciprocating parts, and "rattle" occurs at high speeds. Neither does this allow more economical operation because cut offs earlier than 15% of the stroke are, as said and proved by Sankey, "merely cloaks for exaggerated initial condensation". It is undoubtedly, more economical to reduce steam by the regulator than by working in a cut off earlier than 15%.

'Only in engines having poor valve proportions is the displacement of the piston valve justified. Compared to the best examples of the piston valve-linkage gear class, not only is the fuel and water consumption of the poppet valve-cam gear higher, but the engines thus equipped cannot be "flogged" like those with the older type. In view of this evidence the most that can be done is to return the Scots verdict of "Not proven". The fact remains that the distribution given by well-designed linkage gears to well proportioned long travel valves is unsurpassed in economy and working efficiency for locomotive purposes.

'Two factors determine distribution efficiency. First, good valve and port proportions to avoid undue restriction on admission and to ensure long expansions, short compressions and free exhausts. Second, the ability of the actuating mechanism to maintain the valve in exact phase with the piston, notwithstanding the obliquity effect of the connecting rod, for the piston displacement determines cylinder requirements.'

Caynham Court kept its poppet valves and cylinders until December 1948 when the latter needed renewal and the engine was scrapped.

Oil Burning

Some details of 'Halls' fitted with oil burning apparatus were given in a previous chapter. There were 11 of them and 20 '28xx', five 'Castles' and one '43xx' so treated in the scheme.

In British Railways' day modifications of an experimental nature were noted on a series of forms and a book of progress reports kept. After a time the experiment was concluded and became an approved modification, or was not proceeded with. The final steam locomotive experiment was approved as late as December 1962 and was closed in November 1964 although certain trials involved were not conducted. Only the more interesting experiments are included here and have been abbreviated for reasons of space. It is interesting however to see that there is (as in all engineering) a continuous process of development. Just as it could be difficult, with various types of testing 'on the road' to fit in with normal train running and the acquisition of rolling stock etc, so it was a problem keeping track of modified engines once they were back in traffic. The date in brackets following the experiment indicates the authorisation date.

No W/SW/L/11(8/6/51)

' "Hall" class engine No 7916 with AK boiler to be fitted with 5⅛in dia blast pipe tip with jumper top wedged down. Following complete trials of this locomotive, it was shown that the higher superheat necessitates a blast pipe diameter of 5⅛in instead of 5¼in originally provided for this class with low superheat. With 5⅛in tip, a lower back pressure is obtained for the same power output due to the decrease of density and quantity of exhaust steam. The jumper top appears to fulfil no useful purpose on locomotives superheated 200° and above.'

Trials in service proved satisfactory and 5⅛in tip became standard practice on '69xx' and '79xx' class with three-row superheaters (AK). A new blast pipe was designed, dispensing with the jumper top.

No W/SW/L/40 (17/2/53)

'Improved draughting arrangement on 10 "Hall " class engines with AK boiler. New chimney and blast pipe proportions resulting from Testing Plant experiments. Object to increase steaming capacity of the boiler.'

Engines fitted: Nos 6959/85/87, 7901/19/24/6/7/8/9.

Progress was reported on 19/3/54. 'The authorised 10 engines are now completed, but before proceeding to extend or make standard, financial authority will probably have to be obtained.

'Reports received on seven engines after mileages ranging from 12,000 to 46,000, indicate that they all show good steaming qualities. Comprehensive report on engine No 7919 states that when starting away with a fairly heavy train, the blast on the fire is sharp, but on notching up, this becomes reasonable, although remaining slightly heavier than on engines without modified chimney and blast pipe. Steam pressure is well maintained without the use of the blower. A report on engine No 7927 says that with full regulator and 25% cut off, the boiler with the line steam injector in use maintained full pressure up a 5 miles gradient of 1 in 222 with a load of 259 tons. Reference is made in several reports to the fact that less maintenance to blast pipes is required. Apparently base flange nuts on blast pipes with jumper tops have a tendency to slacken.'

The modification was made standard for AK boilers on 21 July 1954.

No W/SW/L/41 (17/2/53)

'Improved draughting arrangements on 10 "Manor" class engines. New chimney and blast pipe proportions resulting from Testing Plant experiments together with increased air space through grate. Object to increase steaming capacity of boiler'

Engines fitted: Nos 7800/2/3/8/9/23/4/6/7/9.

Progress was reported on 13/3/54. 'Of the 10 engines fitted to date, reports have been received in respect of eight after service varying between two and eight months and these reports speak highly of the steaming qualities of the boiler. The mechanical Foreman at Chester reporting on engines Nos 7800 and 7827 does however, make mention of the "bark" which occurs when notching up and suggests that the bore diameter of the blast pipe top might with advantage be slightly increased. Reports received on the condition of the fire-boxes on four engines, indicate that all are in good condition after two to eight months service.'

The modifications were made standard on 21 July 1954.

No W/SW/L/53 (13/7/53)

'With the object of reducing the number of engine failures due to superheater unit and joint failures, fit seven "Castle", seven "Hall" and six "28xx" class engines with Swindon pattern four tube superheater units. An appropriate number of spare units to be manufactured for replacements.'

Engines fitted: Nos 6956 (1/2/54); 4927 (11/2/54); 4994 (21/4/54); 5034 (23/4/54); 5937 (6/5/54); 4940 (6/5/54); 5014 (6/5/54); 2856 (6/5/54); 5084 (31/5/54); 5011 (31/5/54); 5930 (31/5/54); 4972 (17/6/54); 3865 (27/7/54); 3839 (29/7/54); 2830 (20/8/54); 2849 (20/8/54); 5046 (7/10/54); 2809 (4/10/54); 4076 (25/10/54); 5019 (25/10/54).

Progress was reported on 2 February 1955. 'Early reports indicate that the experimental units are satisfactory in service. Subsequent reports over a period of up to nine months with mileages of up to 45,500, show that there have been no cases reported of joint failures or burst units. In view of the continued difficulties experienced with the old type Swindon pattern superheater joints, and of the apparent success of the new joints and units, it was decided on 20 January 1955 to make the experimental four-tube unit a standard fitting on all boilers at present carrying the old type Swindon unit.'

No W/SW/L/65 (19/10/53)

'Fit improved draughting arrangement on two ''68xx'' (''Grange'') class engines. New chimney and blast pipe proportions resulting from Testing Plant experiments on ''Hall'' class, to increase the steaming capacity of the boiler.'

Engines fitted: Nos 6821 (25/5/54); 6878 (25/5/54).

Progress was reported on 7/12/55. 'Favourable reports from footplate staff in respect of engine No 6878, state that there has been a marked improvement in the steaming qualities of the engine. The steaming of No 6821 is reported as good after 16 months service, with mileage of 68,000. No 6878 stationed at Birkenhead, LMR after 10 months service and 20,000 miles, was reported to be without defect and the steam qualities of the engine were good.'

The modification was made standard on 14/12/55.

No W/SW/L/66 (23/10/53)

'Fit manganese steel liners to the Coupled axleboxes and horns of 20 ''Hall'' class engines with the object of comparing the wear on these liners with that on WR standard bronze liners.'

Engine fitted: No 4936 (22/8/55)

Progress was reported on 24/6/59. 'Engine No 4936 ran 100, 171 miles to H/G repair. Examination found wear over axlebox liners varies from .006in to .012in and on the horn liners from .006in to .012in. The faces of the liners were in good condition, wear being fairly even and only one minor crack had developed. It is considered from these figures of wear that the experimental axlebox liners would give service to a fourth H/G repair, requiring to be ground once during this period which would remove the work hardened surface. The horn liners would give the same length of service but would require to be shimmed and ground at each H/G repair. However in view of the limited labour force available generally for steam locomotive repairs, and the factory repair programme generally, it is considered inopportune at the present time to proceed to fit the outstanding 19 ''Hall'' class engines.'

The experiment was finally officially closed on 7/2/63.

No W/SW/L/68 (11/12/53)

'With the object of generally increasing the efficiency of boiler and engine, fit new tube plates incorporating four-row superheater and 1⅞in diameter boiler tubes in one Standard No 15 boiler as carried by ''10xx'' class engines.'

Engine fitted: No 1009 (6/5/54)

Progress was reported on 6/1/55. 'When this boiler, with pressure reduced to 250lb/sq in was fitted in engine No 1009, modifications were made to the draughting arrangement by fitting double blast pipes 3⅝in dia orifice and a double chimney. Self-cleaning plates were also fitted in the smokebox and a modification made to the valve setting by lengthening the valve

rod 1/16in. Highly successful trials on the Swindon Testing Plant and on the road were carried out by the Loco. Testing Office. The S/15, OB boiler is to be carried by all ''County'' class engines as renewal of fireboxes become necessary. The boiler pressure will be reduced to 250lb/sq in, and double blast pipe and chimney fitted, together with self-cleaning apparatus, only when the OB boiler is used. Modified valve setting by lengthening the valve rod 1/16in to be adopted on all ''County'' class engines, irrespective of boiler carried.'

No W/SW/L/75 (9/2/54)

'Fit six standard No 1 boilers for ''Hall'' class engines, six S/4 and six S/8 boilers with monel metal firebox water space stays throughout, to replace both copper and steel stays of the present arrangement.'

This experiment was cancelled on 9 July 1954 when it was decided as standard practice on Standard boilers No 1, 4, 8 and 12 to replace steel stays with monel metal but retain copper, at heavy repairs.

No W/SW/L/79 (26/2/54)

'Engine No 1000 having the boiler-pressure reduced to 250lb/sq in, to reduce tendency to corking of boiler tubes which results in weeping in tube plate under the higher boiler pressure, was fitted with self-cleaning plates in smokebox, and the blast pipe tips were reduced to 37/16in diameter to improve draughting. In order to effect an improvement in steam distribution and reduce oscillation, the valve rods were lengthened by 1/16in.'

Engine fitted: No 1000 (4/3/54)

Progress was reported on 6/1/55. 'Report from motive power department, shows the experiment to be satisfactory after nine months service. The reduced boiler pressure is considered to have reduced the tendency to corking, and the reduction in diameter of blast pipe tips, together with self-cleaning smokebox apparatus, has almost obviated blocked small tubes. Following the highly successful trials of No 1009 in accordance with experiment W/SW/L/68 the following action is to be taken. S/15, OB boiler is to be carried by all ''County'' class engines as renewal of fireboxes become necessary. The boiler pressure will be reduced to 250lb/sq in, and a double blast pipe and chimney fitted together with self-cleaning apparatus.'

No W/SW/L/93 (18/8/54)

'Fit whistle chains of V14 heavy cadmium plated chain to engines of various classes, to use up the stock of 200ft supplied for experimental purposes, with the object of ascertaining the service life of this chain compared with that of standard knotted type chain at present in use.'

Engines fitted: Nos 1001, 5923, 5947, 5093, 4929, 5044, 1012, 4557, 3771, 9653, 9652, 7743 (all 4/8/54).

Progress was reported on 22/7/55. 'Chains are reported intact and in good condition after 10 months service. Judged on the condition of standard chains which are almost invariably found to be temporarily repaired with wire or string, the experimental chains costing 1d more per engine, can be considered satisfactory.'

No W/SW/L/97 (27/10/54)

'Fit chromium plated piston valve liners, plated by F. B. H.

Durachrome Ltd, as front liners in the steam chest of one '4901' class engine. One liner having a normal finish before plating, fitted in one cylinder, and one liner having a polished surface before plating, in the other cylinder.'

Engine fitted: No 6909 (16/11/54).

Progress was reported on 10/1/56. 'The first two examinations at 5,000 and 14,000 miles respectively, showed that while little wear had occurred on liners, the wear on valve rings was much greater. Before the 2nd examination, the latter were blowing through and were changed. At the 3rd examination (25,500 miles) it was found that little more wear had occurred on liners and that the rate of wear of rings working in plated liners was less than that of rings in unplated liners, attributable to highly polished surfaces of chromium then obtaining. The final examination made at 39,355 miles, showed that the plating was wearing away, as wide bands of cast iron were exposed round the ports. With the front valve heads working mainly on cast iron when in shorter cut-off positions, the wear of valve rings was more even when compared with back valve heads working in unplated liners. Generally considered that increased mileage likely to be obtained from plated liners is largely off-set by reduced mileage obtainable from valve rings. Existing liners to be bored when necessary, but no further chromium plated liners to be fitted.'

The experiment was closed on 10/1/56.

No W/SW/L/98 (11/11/54)

'Fit one S/1 boiler and one S/4 boiler with refractory concrete locomotive fire arch, the firebox seams to be machine rivetted and also the stays behind the brick arch to be rivetted by hand to ensure reliability.'

Engines fitted: Nos 4987 (boiler No 4048), 13/12/54; 9319 (boiler No 6162), 13/12/54.

'The experimental fire arch on engine No 4987 having become unserviceable after little more than one week's service, was replaced by a standard arch. When a portion of the experimental arch approximately 1ft 6in in length broke away, and the remainder of the arch became much reduced in thickness on No 9319, it was replaced by a WR standard arch. This occurred after about two months' service, compared with about four months' service usually obtained from standard arches on the same class engines.

'The experiment is being closed as unsuccessful.'

No W/SW/L/102 (3/1/55)

'To prevent main steam pipe failures, fit both ends of steam pipe between superheater header and cylinders on engine No 1009 with flat faced pipe ends and joint rings.'

Engine fitted: No 1009 (7/1/55)

Progress was reported on 23/8/56. 'The experimental pipe joints proved highly satisfactory during the eighteen months they were under constant observation. Similar joints have subsequently been successfully fitted to other engines of various classes and this type of joint is now made standard on ''King'', ''Castle'', ''County'', ''Hall, ''Grange'' and ''Manor'' classes as engines pass through shops for heavy and other repairs which require the dismantling of steam pipes.'

No W/SW/L/103 (3/1/55)

'Observation of the effect of hydrostatic lubrication in relation to valve and piston wear on engine No 1009, which has a high superheat boiler as the result of incorporating a four row superheater in accordance with experiment W/SW/L/68.'

Engine fitted: No 1009 (7/1/55)

Progress was reported on 10/9/57. 'First examination carried out after 7,330 miles, when the valve rings were renewed, but the piston rings were replaced. The second examination took place after a further 12,500 miles, when the cylinders and pistons showed little wear. The original piston rings were replaced and have now completed a total mileage to date of 19,830. While the valve ring wear was not excessive, it was greater than that on the class 7, but the bush wear was less. Wear figures in general, indicated that the lubrication system for valves and pistons was good. Hydrostatic lubricators should continue to be fitted to all ''10xx'' class engines, irrespective of the degree of superheat, and the experiment closed.'

No W/SW/L/117 (10/8/55, extended 23/10/55)

'Fit both cylinders of one ''4901'' class engine having hydrostatic lubrication and stationed at Swindon motive power depot with BR standard type piston valve heads and steam chest liners to compare the merits of this type of piston valve with that of the WR semi-plug piston valve. Extended to cover a further 20 ''Hall'' class engines.'

Engines fitted: Nos 4953, 27/2/56; 4944, 26/2/57; 6967, 21/5/57; 5990, 29/1/57; 4949, 27/2/57; 5923, 14/2/57; 6955, 13/2/57; 6932, 21/3/57; 4987, 19/2/57; 6962, 13/2/57; 6984, 25/4/57; 5928, 22/6/57; 5905, 15/2/57; 7910, 25/4/57; 5915, 5/7/57; 7918, 27/2/57; 7911, 20/5/57; 6915, 28/6/57; 4984, 5/3/57; 6906, 16/5/57; 4995, 31/7/57.

Progress was reported on 29/5/58. 'After modification to the run of lubrication pipes on No 4953 initial trials were satisfactory and the experiment was extended to cover a further 20 ''Hall'' class engines. Examination carried out on six engines selected for close observation after consecutive mileages of 24,000 showed the general condition of valves and liners to be good and lubrication appeared to be adequate. In three cases the rings were re-fitted for a second period of service and in one case for a third period giving a total mileage of 58,600.

Complaints however were made regarding high frequency vibration on several engines when coasting at speed but other engines similarly fitted were reported satisfactory in this respect. Investigation into this matter resulted in a instruction to increase the supply of oil to valves and cylinders on those engines listed against the experiment fitted with hydrostatic lubrication, but the complaints continued. It has now become clear that only a full scale intensive investigation can finally resolve the matter. In the present circumstances, not withstanding the apparent success in respect of some engines, it is considered that such an investigation should not be proceeded with. The experiment will therefore be concluded.'

Left:
'Mogul' No 6332 fitted with Westinghouse brake pump. At any given time two or three GW locos were air-brake equipped to deal with the through working of air-braked stock from other railways. With the gradual building of dual-braked stock by some 'Big Four' companies, the need for this gear ended. *Photomatic*

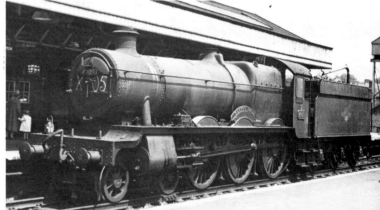

Above:
Churchward tried a number of types of mechanical lubricator but found none adequate for his large diameter, long travel piston valves and developed his own sight feed arrangement. An early mechanical lubricator is seen here attached to No 171 *Albion* which also has the early short cone boiler. *E. Pouteau*

Above right:
No 4905 *Barton Hall* at Southampton Central on 14 June 1961 and fitted with a mechanical lubricator (around 1947). *J. C. Haydon*

Right:
No 2935 *Caynham Court* fitted with poppet valve gear, shown here at Swindon *L&GRP (2042) courtesy David & Charles*

Top right:
No 2935 with a milk train in Sonning Cutting. *M. W. Earley courtesy NRM*

Above right:
Oil Burning No 3952 *Norchliffe Hall* at Birmingham Snow Hill on 16 April 1948 with the 7.05am ex-Paddington. *T. J. Edgington*

Right:
No 3900 *Saint Brides Hall* fitted both with oil burning gear and a turbo-electric lighting rig; at Swindon in June 1949. *T. J. Edgington collection*

Below:
***Saint Brides Hall* again after reversion to coal-firing (and renumbering 4972) at Oxford with a Wolverhampton-Weymouth express. The electric lighting is still fitted in this photograph.** *C. Pearson*

Details of the lighting system –

Top left:
Lights on the back of the tender (No 2918) *Real Photos (13000)*

Top:
Lights conduit and turbo-generator at the front of No 3904. *Real Photos (12998)*

Above:
No 6815 *Frilford Grange* in Swindon Works Yard on 24 January 1953 with a large cover on the side of the smokebox. Its purpose has not been ascertained. *R. C. Riley*

Left:
Layout of switch-box in cab *Real Photos (13001)*

9
What's in the name?

The naming of hundreds of Great Western locomotives after country houses and minor stately-homes has come in for a great deal of criticism by some railway enthusiasts over the years. A printed list may of course look uninspiring but individual engines when seen at work were far better graced with the handsome GW nameplates than being unnamed. It was also very useful in that locomotive types were easily recognisable to all railway grades. (Not *all* railway servants were locomotive enthusiasts!)

Over the years some of the starkness associated with Churchward's earliest engines was gradually mellowed until with the Collett engines they were, to use Westwoods phrase, 'beautiful and quite essentially English'. This continued with Hawksworth; the straight nameplate on the continuous splasher, and flush sided tender of the 'Counties' in their postwar livery all amounted to a handsome machine. His '15xx' 0-6-0PT with outside cylinders and motion showed that Swindon was no where near finished in the aesthetics stakes, and no doubt had not nationalisation interrupted things, more new designs would have appeared.

But to return to our 'Halls', 'Granges' and 'Manors'. Most of their names were of houses on the Great Western system. The owners of these properties were often landowners and farmers, sometimes small shareholders in the GW often important customers; members of the Great Western 'family'. Many names were therefore a silent recognition of this. *They* were of course the people who the company held up their trains for and infuriated and mystified 'strangers'. *They* were the people who were quickly dissuaded from using the railway in such a manner in the 1950s when new brooms swept away all traditions at Paddington and *they* were those who ceased to use the railway and bought cars and lorries, and used their influence in the lobbies to build motorways.

Many of the houses had gardens and woodlands that were opened to the public for charitable purposes. Much of this was arranged under the auspices of 'The Men of the Trees', one of whose Council members was Earl Bathurst a Director of the GWR.

Lists of names built up over the years at Swindon for naming new batches of engines, totalling 399 'Halls', 271 'Manors' and 164 'Granges'. There were therefore quite a few left! The search for names was taken quite seriously at Swindon and some fascinating documents have survived the ravages of time and some extracts follow concerning the Halls of Oxford and Baronial Halls of England; not all names were simply of country houses. Far from being just an endless procession of 'Halls', research into the background to these names leads one into a fascinating byway of English history and geography.

After all the Domesday Book records 9,250 manors, and that in only about 34 of the later English counties. Enough to name a class of Russian standard locomotives!

The Halls of Oxford

These Halls, which generally began as private houses, were for generations the academic homes of the majority of Oxford men. It was in these ancient Halls that the mediaeval university found its strength. In the fifteenth century the Aularian Statutes were issued by which the Halls were governed.

Collegiate discipline was gradually applied to these non collegiate institutions and the majority were either merged into colleges or died out. By the end of the seventeenth century the best days of the Halls had passed away.

Names of some of the early Halls the buildings of which are destroyed and records vanished are: Angle Hall, Ape Hall, Aristotle's Hall, Arthur Hall, Bedel Hall, Bedford Hall, Billyng Hall, Black Hall, Bostar Hall, Broadgate's Hall, Bumell's Inn, Charlton's Inn, Chimney Hall, Corner Hall, Deep Hall, Drawda Hall, Eagle Hall, Elephant Hall, Fragnon Hall, Glassen Hall, Greek Hall, Haberdashers' Hall, Hinksey Hall, Leadenporch Hall, Lion Hall, Maiden Hall, Manger Hall, Peckwater's Inn, Penlow Hall, Perilous Hall, Salisbury Hall, Saracen's Head Hall, St Agatha's Hall, St Catherine's Hall, St Edward's Hall, St Margaret's Hall, St Mary's Hall, St Stephen's Hall, Staple Hall, Studley Hall, Tackley's Inn, Tingewick's Hall, White Hall.

As many as 669 of these Halls have been listed, but it is improbably that more than one-tenth of that number flourished at one time.

The following seven Halls survived Charles I's accession and continued to play a part in University life:

1) **St Alban Hall.** This Hall, regarded as the most ancient that is now in being, owes its name to a family of that name one of whom, an ancient burgher of Oxford living in King John's time and afterwards, was called 'Robertus de Sancto Albano'.

It has always been connected with Merton College – whose property the premises became soon after the Dissolution. Its principals were for years Merton students, and eventually in 1882 in pursuance of Statutes framed by the Oxford University Commissioners, the Hall was annexed to Merton College.

2) **St Mary's Hall.** This Hall was founded by junior members of Oriel College before they became eligible, according to the first statutes, to enter the College itself. It has always been connected with Oriel College until in 1902 it lost its independence and was annexed to the College.

William (afterwards Cardinal) Allen was Principal in Queen Mary's time – and to this great Englishman the preservation of the Catholic religion in England was largely due. Its students include the great Sir Thomas More.

The buildings date from the seventeenth century except a portion of the wall on the south side of the quadrangle, which is of the 15th century.

3) **St Edmund Hall.** Generally agreed, notwithstanding the contrary opinion of Wood, that St Edmund Hall derived its name

from Edmund Le Riche, Archbishop of Canterbury, who delivered lectures in certain schools on the same site from 1219 to 1226 and was soon after his death canonised. The 16th of November, the day set apart for him in the Romish calender, was formerly kept as a 'gaudy' by members of the Halls.

In 1269 the property was presented by Thomas de Malmesbury, Vicar of Cowley, to the Abbey of Oseney, but continued to be let for the use of students. In 1557 the property was acquired by Queen's College, and from then onwards Queen's men repeatedly presided over the Hall. Wood carries the list of Principals back to 1317. At the end of the nineteenth century when all the other Halls were being annexed by colleges, St Edmund Hall was nearly annexed by Queen's, but under Dr Moore the vitality of the Society swerved, and in 1914 the statute for preserving the Hall's independence received the assent of the Crown.

4) **Gloucester Hall.** This Hall was founded in 1283 by William Giffard, Baron of Brimsfield in Gloucestershire, for Benedictine monks at first chosen exclusively from the monastery of St Peter at Gloucester, but later extended to students from any Benedictine House.

In the 16th century it was chiefly a resort of Oxford men who adhered to the old faith, and became a refuge for Catholics. The site is now occupied and the premises incorporated in Worcester College.

5) **Hart Hall.** One of the little group of Halls, which, at the end of the 13th century, stood on the site of Hertford College. Its name was taken from a certain Elias of Hertford who seems to have bought a house in Oxford in 1283 and to have let it out to clerks as an investment. A hart's head – the device he used – suggested a name for the Hall and arms later for the College. The Hall passed eventually from Elias' son to Bishop Stapledon. It was connected with New College – many of the principals and students being New College men, but during the 15th and 16th centuries it was ruled and managed chiefly by Exeter men.

6) **Magdalen Hall.** The name first bestowed on the earliest home of Waynflete's scholars was applied from the beginning of the 16th century to the Grammar Hall and the buildings around it which grew up outside the gates of Magdalen College. Magdalen College owned the site of the Hall and supplied most of the principals, but it had no jurisdiction over the Hall students.

About 1600 the Hall became more popular than the College. John Wilkinson, appointed Principal in 1605 carried its fortunes to the highest point, and under his management Exhibitions for students were created and new quarters built. Of these, only the picturesque little building known as the Grammar Hall survives. Wilkinson's nephew was the next principal, and the Hall became the chief seminary in the University. The Society was most prosperous under the two Wilkinsons and continued to flourish till 1820 when a destructive fire consumed about half of the apartments of the students.

7) **New Inn Hall.** This was a smaller society than the previous ones, but survived with some of its venerable buildings into recent times. Christopher Rogers, appointed Principal in 1626, a leading Puritan in the University is said to have 'fled to the Parliamentary Party' – his students apparently deserted too, and the King established his mint in their empty quarters. From 1630-1648 this Hall, like Magdalen Hall, was a Puritan centre.

In 1887 the Hall was annexed to Balliol College, but about 1897 most of the buildings were sold by Balliol and were remodelled for the purposes of Hannington Memorial Hall.

By the end of the 19th century the old Halls had almost disappeared.

Of the mediaeval halls which lasted on into the 17th century – four had already developed into Colleges after 1874 only four survived, and the later Commissioners settled their fate. All but one were absorbed into Colleges.

Only St Edmund Hall maintained an independent position and could claim to be the 'linear survivor of a system older than any college and to represent the ancient Halls where the mediaeval students gathered'.

'49xx' class engines named after Oxford Halls

Ripon Hall [5914] Founded in Ripon in 1898 by Rt Rev Bishop Boyd Carpenter, but moved to Oxford in 1919. Only University graduates are eligible for admission, with certain exceptions.

It is licensed as a place of residence for ordinands desiring to take the Honours School of Theology and the Diploma in Theology at Oxford University. It is now situated on Boar's Hill, just outside Oxford, in the buildings which were formerly the residence of the Earl of Berkeley (and known as Berkeley Castle) and which is said to have been a copy of the other Berkeley Castle in Gloucestershire.

Wycliffe Hall [5920] Opened in 1877-78 and enlarged in 1881. It is a Theological Hall for graduates desiring to prepare for ordinations.

Campion Hall [5941] In 1896 the Rev R. F. Clarke of Trinity College Oxford obtained licence to open a Private Hall for members of the Society of Jesus (Jesuits). In 1915 the Rev. C. D. Plater became Master and during his Mastership the Hall was given the status of a Permanent Private Hall. New buildings were built in Brewer Street, Oxford on the site of the old Micklem Hall, for many years a well known University lodging-house where many distinguished people have lodged during their residence in Oxford.

St Benet's Hall [5947] The foundation dates from 1897 when the English Benedictine Abbey of Ampleforth in Yorkshire opened a house of studies for members of its community at Oxford. It became a Permanent Private Hall in 1918.

St Edmund Hall [5960] This is now the only survivor of that type of academical society which first provided for the residence of scholars coming to the University. The ancient association with the name of St Edmund of Abingdon, Archbishop of Canterbury, is traditionally supposed to commemorate the fact that St Edmund, when he was teaching in the University, was sometime resident in a house on this site. The Hall was owned by clerks of the family of Bermingham before 1238 and then came into the possession of Oseney Abbey about 1270 and at the time of the dissolution of the Abbey it was sold.

Later it was sold again and purchased by W. Denyse, Provost of the Queen's College Oxford in 1553 and thus the connexion between the college and the Hall which had been growing since the beginning of the 15th century was confirmed and in 1559 it was agreed by the University and the College that Queen's College should have the perpetual right of electing the Principal of the Hall.

Frewin Hall [6906] This was originally an Augustinian Friary erected in 1414 on the site of earlier buildings, whose 12th century cellars still remain, at the back of Cornmarket Street. It is celebrated as the abode of His Majesty King Edward VII when as Prince of Wales he was in residence in Oxford in 1860-61.

The older part of the house has good Elizabethan panelling and roofs, and the large carriage entrance in New Inn Hall street is mediaeval and has at its side two arches of the monastic cloisters. It was occupied for nearly a hundred years in the 18th and 19th centuries by successive Regius Professors of Medicine.

St Peter's Hall [7900] Opened in 1928 as a memorial to the late Francis James Chavasse D.D., formerly Bishop of Liverpool; sometime Principal of Wycliffe Hall and Rector of St Peter-le-Bailey, Oxford. The buildings include the parochial buildings of St Peter-le-Bailey and part of old New Inn Hall. It ranks as a Permanent Private Hall in the University of Oxford.

Lady Margaret Hall [7911] This Hall was founded in 1878, and opened in 1879. It was the first Permanent Hall for the education of women in the University of Oxford. The first Principal was Dame Elizabeth Wordsworth, a great-niece of the famous poet.

Some Baronial Halls of England

Blackwell Hall [6996] Formerly stood on the site of the Guildhall, London from 1356-1820.

Brocket Hall [5987] Built in 1500 and passed through the hands of four generations of Brockets. It was the residence of Lord Melbourne for some time; Queen Victoria visited him there in 1841.

Heveningham Hall [7909] In Suffolk, this was built in the early 18th century by Sir John Heveningham.

Kirby Hall [5993] Northamptonshire (now deserted). Seat of the Hattons and built by Humphrey Stafford, 6th Earl of Northampton in 1570.

Wollaton Hall [5999] Nottinghamshire. Was erected by Sir Francis Willoughby in the 16th century.

Benthall Hall [6995] Shropshire. Built in 1535.

Aston Hall [4986] Erected during the reign of James I although it is held that a baronial mansion existed on the site previous to the present one, about three centuries earlier. Was the residence of James Watt, son of the inventor.

Pitchford Hall [4953] About six miles from Shrewsbury, was built in the reign of Henry VIII. Was visited in 1832 by Queen Victoria (then a Princess).

Trentham Hall [5915] Staffordshire, was built in the 15th century and occupied by the Duke of Suffolk during the reign of King Henry VIII. To Marquis of Stafford in 1786.

Helmingham Hall [6947] Built in the 16th century in Suffolk it is the seat of the family of Tollemache. Queen Elizabeth I stayed at the house in 1561 and is said to be godmother to one of the children.

Hengrave Hall [5970] Suffolk, built 1525-1538.

Preservation

At the time of writing (1983) the following locomotives relevant to this book are still in existence:

'43xx' class 2-6-0

5322	(8322 from 1/28 to 6/44)	Didcot Railway Centre
9303	(7325 from 6/58)	Severn Valley Railway

'4901' class 4-6-0 'Hall'

4920	Dumbleton Hall	Dart Valley Railway
4930	Hagley Hall	Severn Valley Railway
4936	Kinlet Hall	Peak Railway, Matlock
4942	Maindy Hall	Didcot Railway Centre
4953	Pitchford Hall	Dean Forest Railway
4979	Wootton Hall	Barry
4983	Albert Hall	Birmingham Railway Museum

5900	Hinderton Hall	Didcot Railway Centre
5952	Cogan Hall	Gloucestershire-Warwickshire Railway
5967	Bickmarsh Hall	Barry
5972	Olton Hall	Procor Ltd, Wakefield

'6959' class 4-6-0 'Modified Hall'

6960	Raveningham Hall	Severn Valley Railway
6984	Owsden Hall	Barry
6989	Wightwick Hall	Quainton Railway Centre
6990	Witherslack Hall	Great Central Railway
6998	Burton Agnes Hall	Didcot Railway Centre
7903	Foremarke Hall	Swindon & Cricklade Railway
7927	Willington Hall	Barry

'78xx' class 4-6-0 'Manor'

7802	Bradley Manor	Severn Valley Railway
7808	Cookham Manor	Didcot Railway Centre
7812	Erlestoke Manor	Severn Valley Railway
7819	Hinton Manor	Severn Valley Railway
7820	Dinmore Manor	Gwili Railway
7821	Ditcheat Manor	Gloucestershire-Warwickshire Railway
7822	Foxcote Manor	Cambrian Railways Society, Oswestry
7827	Lydham Manor	Torbay & Dartmouth Railway
7828	Odney Manor	Gloucestershire-Warwickshire Railway

The story of Great Western preservation has been told very fully and affectionately in Brian Hollingsworth's *Great Western Adventure*.[34]

It is unfortunate that none of these mixed traffic classes are represented in the National Collection. The only GW two-cylinder locomotive in the collection is one of the 2-8-0s, No 2818. These were superb machines of course and were never really improved upon. Tests in normal service in the 1950s showed very low specific coal consumption – lower than any other equivalent type. In 1906 No 2808 while still saturated hauled a train of 2,012 tons from Swindon to Acton. It was 1967 before another locomotive managed such a feat; the prototype diesel-electric *Kestrel*.

Below:
No 6801 *Aylburton Grange* **on Swindon dump 6 December 1960. This was the first 'Grange' to be condemned.** *R. C. Riley*

Top left:
Typical nameplates *Saint Martin* (4900) – the prototype 'Hall' taken at Old Oak Common on 23 September 1956. *R. C. Riley*

Top:
Hurst Grange (6851). *R. C. Riley*

Above:
Hook Norton Manor (7823) taken at Laira on 15 July 1956. *R. C. Riley*

Left:
Now is the winter of our discontent. A forlorn selection of 'Halls' and 'Granges' at Oxford on 15 January 1966. The Western Region had by this time been completely dieselised. *L. A. Nixon*

In spite of the saving of many GWR two-cylinder 4-6-0s by preservation groups, many restored from scrap, the stocks at Barry ensured that many latecomers to the preservation scheme have had something to aim at. Although these schemes are looking on with scepticism in some quarters it is amazing how much has been done

Below left:
No 5952 *Cogan Hall* arrives on the Gloucester & Warwickshire Railway. *P. Nicholson*

Top:
No 4930 *Hagley Hall* on the 'Welsh Marches Express' south of Hereford on 14 February 1981.
Rex Coffin

Above:
The following year *Hagley Hall* again, this time with the SLOA Pullman set and a train of elevated status, no mere 'express' – the 'Welsh Marches Pullman'. *Ken Bull*

Right:
No 7812 *Erlestoke Manor* piloting *Hagley Hall* on the climb to Llanvihangel on the northbound 'Welsh Marches Pullman' on 17 April 1982. *P. G. Green*

Above:
Enthusiasts specials were run in normal steam days; here No 7929 *Wyke Hall* (the last of the class) pilots No 72008 *Clan McLeod* near Swan Village with a Derbyshire Railway Society special to Tyseley and Wolverhampton on 24 March 1963. *G. England*

Left:
No 7808 *Cookham Manor* on an SLS special at Marlborough on 10 September 1961. *T. J. Edgington*

Below:
No 6859 *Yiewsley Grange* on a RCTS/SLS special special at Swansea High Street on 26 September 1965. *T. J. Edgington*

Top:
The Great Western Society has been a pioneer in the setting up of a live steam centre and museum devoted to one company. Here an array of three 4-6-0s has been set up for photographers at a Didcot open day. Nos 5900 *Hinderton Hall,* 7808 *Cookham Manor* and 6998 *Burton Agnes Hall.* *GWS*

Above:
No 7808 *Cookham Manor* poses on the turntable at Didcot Railway Centre. *GWS*

Right:
For the Stockton & Darlington 150 celebrations the GWS sent *Cookham Manor* and also *Shannon* from the Wantage Tramway (on loan from the National Collection). Here No 7808 heads away from Eaglescliffe towards Stockton with preserved GW stock, a brown Siphon 'G' leading. 11 August 1975. *I. S. Carr*

Above:
The GWS 'Halls' shunting vintage stock including this Ocean Special Saloon at Dorridge after one vehicle had developed a hot box, 15 May 1976. *P. H. Hanson*

Left:
No 6998 *Burton Agnes Hall* pilots 0-4-2T No 1466 on the GWS special train from Plymouth to Didcot on 2 December 1967. The train is seen here ascending Dainton Bank. *Patrick Russell*

Below:
No 5900 *Hinderton Hall* awaiting departure at Leamington Spa on 3 March 1979. *John Titlow*

Bottom:
Another night shot of the same locomotive, this time at the buffers at Paddington two days previously. Let us hope this sight will be a periodic experience for many years to come. *Brian Stephenson*

Further Reading

K. J. Cook: The late G. J. Churchward's Locomotive Development on the GWR (I. Loco. E. 1950. Paper no. 492)

K. J. Cook: *Swindon Steam 1921-51* (Ian Allan, 1974)

Brian Haresnape: *Collett and Hawksworth Locomotives* (Ian Allan, 1978)

H. Holcroft: *An Outline of Great Western Locomotive Practice 1837-1947* (Ian Allan, 1957)

O. S. Nock: *The GWR Mixed Traffic 4-6-0s* (Patrick Stephens, 1983)

O. S. Nock: *GWR Steam* (David & Charles, 1972)

E. J. Nutty: *GWR Two-Cylinder Piston Valve Steam Locomotives* (E. J. Nutty & Sons, 1977)

R.C.T.S.: *Locomotives of the Great Western Railway*
    Part 8 Modern Passenger Classes (1960)
    Part 9 Standard Two-Cylinder Classes (1962)
    Part 12 A Chronological & Statistical Survey (1974)
    Part 13 Preservation and Supplementary Information (1983)

W. A. Tuplin: *Great Western Steam* (Allen & Unwin, 1958, 1965)

W. A. Tuplin: *Great Western Saints and Sinners* (Allen & Unwin, 1971)

References and Notes

(References in the text are not repeated.)

Chapter 1
1 The exception is to be found in Chapter 4 of H. A. V. Bulleid *Master Builders of Steam* (Ian Allan 1963 and 1984). This very readable account is however all too brief.
2 Sir Monty Finniston *The Terotechnology Way to Save BSC £100 Million (Engineer*, 20 March 1975).
3 J. N. Westwood *Locomotive Designers in the Age of Steam* (Sidgwick & Jackson 1977).
4 Lanchester, although of a different temperament and background, and showing a different approach, shared similar problems with Churchward. The latter had the mechanical engineering department of a railway company to keep running whilst introducing his new order. Lanchester was continually pressed by his directors (who were also his backers) to produce a marketable commodity even at the expense of his basic ideas. In his case, in the long term, his backers won the argument.
5 P. W. Kingsford *F. W. Lanchester: A Life of an Engineer* (Edward Arnold 1960)

Chapter 2
6 Sir William Stanier *George Jackson Churchward, Chief Mechanical Engineer, Great Western Railway. (Trans Newcomen Society Vol XXX 1955)*
7 L. Lawrence. Letter to the Editor *(Railway Gazette 16 July 1943)*
8 H. Holcroft. Letter to the Editor *(Engineer 1947 Vol)*
9 Campbell Highet *All Steamed Up!* (Oxford Publishing Co 1975)
10 See Appendix 1
11 H. Holcroft *The Institution of Locomotive Engineers (Railway Gazette 12 May 1961)*
12 Prof. Ivo Kolin *150th Anniversary of the Carnot Cycle (Engineering February 1975)*

Chapter 3
13 These reference numbers are to a series of small diagrams issued with the reports to the Board. They have not been reproduced here but a photograph appears of each class.

Chapter 4
14 Anon. *New Sentinel Locomotives for South America (Railway Gazette 15 June 1934)*
15 Anon. *Six-engined Sentinel Steam Locomotives for Colombia (Locomotive 14 July 1934)*

Chapter 5
16 Brian Reed *Modern Railway Motive Power* (Temple Press 1950)

Chapter 6
17 T. J. Tarrant *Notes on Running Shed Practice* (Trans Swindon Engineering Society, 1949. Paper No 221)
18 Colin Jacks *Drawn by Steam* (Bradford Barton)
19 Harold Gasson. *Footplate Days: More Reminiscences of a Great Western Fireman* (Oxford Pub Co 1978)
20 R. S. Potts *Twenty Years at Tyseley (Steam Alive! Trains Illustrated No 9)*
21 See especially O. S. Nock *Sixty Years of Western Express Running* (2nd edition, Ian Allan, 1973)

Chapter 7
22 G. V. Lomonosoff *Problems of Railway Mechanics (Proc. I. Mech. E. 1931)*
23 Anthony Hyman *Charles Babbage: Pioneer of the Computer* (Oxford University Press 1982)
24 D. K. Clark *Railway Machinery* (Blackie & Son 1855)
25 D. R. Carling *Locomotive Testing Stations (Trans Newcomen Society XLV 1972-3)*
26 J. N. Westwood *Soviet Locomotive Technology during Industrialisation 1928-52* (Macmillan 1982)
27 Anon. *Locomotive Testing Plant at Swindon (Engineer 1905 Vol 100)*
The original set up was to be a number of test beds (four) which fed the works compressed air supply by using compressors as load. New or overhauled locomotives would be run-in and supply compressed air at the same time.
28 S. O. Ell *BR-WR Outline of WR Methods of Locomotive Testing for Determination of Fuel Consumption Relative to the Drawbar Characteristics* (BR Swindon 1952 – internal document)
29 S. O. Ell *Developments in Locomotive Testing (J. I. Loco. E. 1953. Paper no. 527)*
30 C. Rous-Marten *French Compounds on the Great Western Railway (Engineer 1906 – Part 1)*
31 C. J. Allen *Locomotive Practice and Performance. (Railway Magazine 1923)*
32 C. J. Allen *Locomotive Practice and Performance (Railway Magazine 1934)*

Chapter 8
33 S. O. Ell *The Steam Distribution of the Four-Cylinder Engine* (Swindon Engineering Society 1933)

Chapter 9
34 Brian Hollingsworth *Great Western Adventure* (David & Charles 1981)

Appendices
I
Names and Numbers

'Hall' Class

No	Name	Date Built	Date Withdrawn	Notes	No	Name	Date Built	Date Withdrawn	Notes
4900	Saint Martin	12/24	4/59	5	4947	Nanhoran Hall	8/29	9/62	
4901	Adderley Hall	12/28	9/60		4948	Northwick Hall	8/29	9/62	
4902	Aldenham Hall	12/28	9/63		4949	Packwood Hall	8/29	9/64	
4903	Astley Hall	12/28	10/64		4950	Patshull Hall	8/29	5/64	
4904	Binnegar Hall	12/28	12/63		4951	Pendeford Hall	7/29	6/64	
4905	Barton Hall	12/28	11/63		4952	Peplow Hall	8/29	9/62	
4906	Bradfield Hall	1/29	9/62		4953	Pitchford Hall	8/29	5/63	
4907	Broughton Hall	1/29	8/63		4954	Plaish Hall	8/29	11/64	
4908	Broome Hall	1/29	10/63		4955	Plaspower Hall	8/29	10/63	
4909	Blakesley Hall	1/29	9/62		4956	Plowden Hall	9/29	7/63	
4910	Blaisdon Hall	1/29	12/63		4957	Postlip Hall	9/29	3/62	
4911	Bowden Hall	2/29	6/41		4958	Priory Hall	9/29	9/64	
4912	Berrington Hall	2/29	8/62		4959	Purley Hall	9/29	12/64	
4913	Baglan Hall	2/29	9/62		4960	Pyle Hall	9/29	9/62	
4914	Cranmore Hall	2/29	12/63		4961	Pyrland Hall	11/29	11/62	
4915	Condover Hall	2/29	2/63		4962	Ragley Hall	11/29	10/65	
4916	Crumlin Hall	2/29	8/64		4963	Rignall Hall	11/29	6/62	
4917	Crosswood Hall	3/29	9/62		4964	Rodwell Hall	11/29	10/63	
4918	Dartington Hall	3/29	6/63		4965	Rood Ashton Hall	11/29	3/62	
4919	Donnington Hall	3/29	10/64		4966	Shakenhurst Hall	11/29	11/63	
4920	Dumbleton Hall	3/29	12/65		4967	Shirenewton Hall	12/29	9/62	
4921	Eaton Hall	4/29	9/62		4968	Shotton Hall	12/29	7/62	
4922	Enville Hall	4/29	7/63		4969	Shrugborough Hall	12/29	9/62	
4923	Evenley Hall	4/29	5/64		4970	Sketty Hall	12/29	7/63	
4924	Eydon Hall	5/29	10/63		4971	Stanway Hall	1/30	8/62	
4925	Eynsham Hall	5/29	8/62		4972	Saint Brides Hall	1/30	2/64	1
4926	Fairleigh Hall	5/29	9/61		4973	Sweeney Hall	1/30	7/62	
4927	Farnborough Hall	5/29	9/63		4974	Talgarth Hall	1/30	4/62	
4928	Gatacre Hall	5/29	12/63		4975	Umberslade Hall	1/30	9/63	
4929	Goytrey Hall	5/29	3/65		4976	Warfield Hall	1/30	5/64	
4930	Hagley Hall	5/29	12/63		4977	Watcombe Hall	1/30	5/62	
4931	Hanbury Hall	5/29	7/62		4978	Westwood Hall	2/30	9/64	
4932	Hatherton Hall	6/29	11/64		4979	Wootton Hall	2/30	12/63	
4933	Himley Hall	6/29	8/64		4980	Wrottesley Hall	2/30	7/63	
4934	Hindlip Hall	6/29	9/62		4981	Abberley Hall	12/30	10/63	
4935	Ketley Hall	6/29	3/63		4982	Acton Hall	1/31	5/62	
4936	Kinlet Hall	6/29	1/64		4983	Albert Hall	1/31	12/63	
4937	Lanelay Hall	6/29	9/62		4984	Albrighton Hall	1/31	9/62	
4938	Liddington Hall	6/29	11/62		4985	Allesley Hall	1/31	9/64	2
4939	Littleton Hall	7/29	2/63		4986	Aston Hall	1/31	5/62	
4940	Ludford Hall	7/29	11/59		4987	Brockley Hall	1/31	4/62	
4941	Llangedwyn Hall	7/29	10/62		4988	Bulwell Hall	1/31	2/64	
4942	Maindy Hall	7/29	12/63		4989	Cherwell Hall	2/31	11/64	
4943	Marrington Hall	7/29	12/63		4990	Clifton Hall	2/31	4/62	
4944	Middleton Hall	7/29	9/62		4991	Cobham Hall	2/31	12/63	
4945	Milligan Hall	8/29	11/61		4992	Crosby Hall	2/31	4/65	
4946	Moseley Hall	8/29	6/63		4993	Dalton Hall	2/31	2/65	
					4994	Downton Hall	2/31	3/63	

No	Name	Date Built	Date Withdrawn	Notes	No	Name	Date Built	Date Withdrawn	Notes
4995	Easton Hall	2/31	6/62		5956	Horsley Hall	12/35	3/63	
4996	Eden Hall	3/31	9/63		5957	Hutton Hall	12/35	7/64	
4997	Elton Hall	3/31	10/61		5958	Knolton Hall	1/36	3/64	
4998	Eyton Hall	3/31	10/63		5959	Mawley Hall	1/36	9/62	
4999	Gopsal Hall	3/31	9/62		5960	Saint Edmund Hall	1/36	9/62	
5900	Hinderton Hall	3/31	12/63	7	5961	Toynbee Hall	6/35	8/65	
5901	Hazel Hall	5/31	6/64		5962	Wantage Hall	7/36	11/64	7
5902	Howick Hall	5/31	11/62		5963	Wimpole Hall	7/36	6/64	
5903	Keele Hall	5/31	9/63		5964	Wolseley Hall	7/36	9/62	7
5904	Kelham Hall	5/31	11/63		5965	Woollas Hall	8/36	7/62	
5905	Knowsley Hall	5/31	7/63	7	5966	Ashford Hall	3/37	9/62	
5906	Lawton Hall	5/31	5/62		5967	Bickmarsh Hall	3/37	6/64	7
5907	Marble Hall	5/31	11/61		5968	Cory Hall	3/37	9/62	
5908	Moreton Hall	6/31	7/63		5969	Honington Hall	4/37	8/62	
5909	Newton Hall	6/31	7/62		5970	Hengrave Hall	4/37	11/63	
5910	Park Hall	6/31	9/62		5971	Merevale Hall	4/37	12/65	
5911	Preston Hall	6/31	9/62		5972	Olton Hall	4/37	12/63	7
5912	Queen's Hall	6/31	12/62	3	5973	Rolleston Hall	5/37	9/62	
5913	Rushton Hall	6/31	5/62		5974	Wallsworth Hall	4/37	12/64	7
5914	Ripon Hall	7/31	1/64		5975	Winslow Hall	5/37	7/64	
5915	Trentham Hall	7/31	1/60		5976	Ashwicke Hall	9/38	7/64	
5916	Trinity Hall	7/31	7/62		5977	Beckford Hall	9/38	8/63	7
5917	Westminster Hall	7/31	9/62		5978	Bodinnick Hall	9/38	10/63	7
5918	Walton Hall	7/31	9/62		5979	Cruckton Hall	9/38	11/64	7
5919	Worsley Hall	7/31	8/63		5980	Dingley Hall	9/38	9/62	
5920	Wycliffe Hall	8/31	1/62		5981	Frensham Hall	10/38	9/62	
5921	Bingley Hall	5/33	1/62		5982	Harrington Hall	10/38	9/62	
5922	Caxton Hall	5/33	1/64		5983	Henley Hall	10/38	4/65	
5923	Colston Hall	5/33	12/63		5984	Linden Hall	10/38	1/65	
5924	Dinton Hall	5/33	12/63		5985	Mostyn Hall	10/38	9/63	7
5925	Eastcote Hall	5/33	10/62		5986	Arbury Hall	11/39	9/63	
5926	Grotrian Hall	6/33	9/62		5987	Brocket Hall	11/39	1/64	
5927	Guild Hall	6/63	10/64		5988	Bostock Hall	11/39	10/65	
5928	Haddon Hall	6/33	5/62		5989	Cransley Hall	12/39	7/62	
5929	Hanham Hall	6/33	10/63		5990	Dorford Hall	12/39	1/65	
5930	Hannington Hall	6/33	9/62		5991	Gresham Hall	12/39	7/64	
5931	Hatherley Hall	6/33	9/62		5992	Horton Hall	12/39	8/65	
5932	Haydon Hall	6/33	10/65		5993	Kirby Hall	12/39	5/63	
5933	Kingsway Hall	6/33	8/65		5994	Roydon Hall	12/39	3/63	
5934	Kneller Hall	6/33	5/64		5995	Wick Hall	1/40	4/63	
5935	Norton Hall	7/33	5/62		5996	Mytton Hall	6/40	8/62	
5936	Oakley Hall	7/33	1/65		5997	Sparkford Hall	6/40	7/62	
5937	Stanford Hall	7/33	11/63		5998	Trevor Hall	6/40	3/64	
5938	Stanley Hall	7/33	5/63		5999	Wollaton Hall	6/40	9/62	7
5939	Tangley Hall	7/33	10/64		6900	Abney Hall	6/40	10/64	
5940	Whitbourne Hall	8/33	9/62		6901	Arley Hall	7/40	6/64	
5941	Campion Hall	2/35	7/62	7	6902	Butlers Hall	7/40	5/61	7
5942	Doldowlod Hall	2/35	12/63		6903	Belmont Hall	7/40	9/65	
5943	Elmdon Hall	3/35	6/63		6904	Charfield Hall	7/40	1/65	7
5944	Ickenham Hall	3/35	4/63		6905	Claughton Hall	7/40	6/64	
5945	Leckhampton Hall	3/35	4/63		6906	Chicheley Hall	11/40	4/65	
5946	Marwell Hall	3/35	7/62		6907	Davenham Hall	11/40	2/65	7
5947	Saint Benet's Hall	3/35	7/62		6908	Downham Hall	11/40	7/65	
5948	Siddington Hall	3/35	8/63		6909	Frewin Hall	11/40	6/64	
5949	Trematon Hall	4/35	5/61		6910	Gossington Hall	12/40	10/65	7
5950	Wardley Hall	4/35	11/61	7	6911	Holker Hall	1/41	4/65	
5951	Clyffe Hall	12/35	4/64		6912	Helmster Hall	1/41	2/64	7
5952	Cogan Hall	12/35	6/64	7	6913	Levens Hall	2/41	6/64	7
5953	Dunley Hall	12/35	10/62		6914	Langton Hall	2/41	4/64	7
5954	Faendre Hall	12/35	10/63		6915	Mursley Hall	2/41	2/65	
5955	Garth Hall	12/35	4/65		6916	Misterton Hall	6/41	8/65	4

No	Name	Date Built	Date Withdrawn	Notes
6917	*Oldlands Hall*	6/41	9/65	4.7
6918	*Sandon Hall*	6/41	6/65	4.7
6919	*Tylney Hall*	6/41	8/63	4.7
6920	*Barningham Hall*	7/41	12/63	4
6921	*Borwick Hall*	7/41	10/65	4.7
6922	*Burton Hall*	7/41	4/65	4.7
6923	*Croxteth Hall*	7/41	12/65	4.7
6924	*Grantley Hall*	8/41	10/65	4
6925	*Hackness Hall*	8/41	11/64	4
6926	*Holkham Hall*	11/41	5/65	4
6927	*Lilford Hall*	11/41	10/65	4
6928	*Underley Hall*	11/41	6/65	4
6929	*Whorlton Hall*	11/41	10/63	4
6930	*Aldersey Hall*	11/41	10/65	4
6931	*Aldborough Hall*	12/41	10/65	4.7
6932	*Burwarton Hall*	12/41	12/65	4
6933	*Birtles Hall*	12/41	11/64	4
6934	*Beachamwell Hall*	12/41	10/65	4.7
6935	*Browsholme Hall*	12/41	2/65	4
6936	*Breccles Hall*	7/42	11/64	4.7
6937	*Conyngham Hall*	7/42	12/65	4.7
6938	*Corndean Hall*	7/42	3/63	4.7
6939	*Calveley Hall*	7/42	10/63	4
6940	*Didlington Hall*	8/42	5/64	4
6941	*Fillongley Hall*	8/42	4/64	4.7
6942	*Eshton Hall*	8/42	12/64	4
6943	*Farnley Hall*	8/42	12/63	4.7
6944	*Fledborough Hall*	9/42	11/65	4.7
6945	*Glasfryn Hall*	9/42	9/64	4.7
6946	*Heatherden Hall*	12/42	6/64	4
6947	*Helmingham Hall*	12/42	11/65	4.7
6948	*Holbrooke Hall*	12/42	12/63	4
6949	*Haberfield Hall*	12/42	5/61	4
6950	*Kingsthorpe Hall*	12/42	6/64	4
6951	*Impney Hall*	2/43	12/65	4.7
6952	*Kimberley Hall*	2/43	12/65	4.7
6953	*Leighton Hall*	2/43	12/65	4
6954	*Lotherton Hall*	3/43	5/64	4.7
6955	*Lydcott Hall*	3/43	2/65	4.7
6956	*Mottram Hall*	3/43	12/65	4
6957	*Norcliffe Hall*	4/43	10/65	4.7
6958	*Oxburgh Hall*	4/43	6/65	4.7

'Modified Hall' Class

No	Name	Date Built	Date Withdrawn	Notes
6959	*Peatling Hall*	3/44	12/65	4
6960	*Raveningham Hall*	3/44	6/64	4
6961	*Stedham Hall*	3/44	9/65	4
6962	*Soughton Hall*	4/44	1/63	4
6963	*Throwley Hall*	4/44	7/65	4
6964	*Thornbridge Hall*	5/44	9/65	4
6965	*Thirlestaine Hall*	7/44	10/65	4
6966	*Witchingham Hall*	5/44	9/64	4
6967	*Willesley Hall*	8/44	12/65	4
6968	*Woodcock Hall*	9/44	9/63	4
6969	*Wraysbury Hall*	9/44	2/65	4
6970	*Whaddon Hall*	9/44	6/64	4
6971	*Athelhampton Hall*	10/47	10/64	
6972	*Beningbrough Hall*	10/47	3/64	
6973	*Bricklehampton Hall*	10/47	8/65	
6974	*Bryngwyn Hall*	10/47	5/65	
6975	*Capesthorne Hall*	10/47	12/63	
6976	*Graythwaite Hall*	10/47	10/65	
6977	*Grundisburgh Hall*	11/47	12/63	
6978	*Haroldstone Hall*	11/47	7/65	
6979	*Helperly Hall*	11/47	2/65	
6980	*Llanrumney Hall*	11/47	10/65	
6981	*Marbury Hall*	2/48	3/64	
6982	*Melmerby Hall*	1/48	8/64	
6983	*Otterington Hall*	2/48	8/65	
6984	*Owsden Hall*	2/48	12/65	
6985	*Parwick Hall*	2/48	9/64	
6986	*Rydal Hall*	3/48	4/65	
6987	*Shervington Hall*	3/48	9/64	
6988	*Swithland Hall*	3/48	9/64	
6989	*Wightwick Hall*	3/48	6/64	
6990	*Witherslack Hall*	4/48	12/65	
6991	*Acton Burnell Hall*	11/48	12/65	
6992	*Arborfield Hall*	11/48	6/64	
6993	*Arthog Hall*	12/48	12/65	
6994	*Baggrave Hall*	12/48	11/64	
6995	*Benthall Hall*	12/48	3/65	
6996	*Blackwell Hall*	1/49	10/64	
6997	*Bryn-Ivor Hall*	1/49	11/64	
6998	*Burton Agnes Hall*	1/49	12/65	
6999	*Capel Dewi Hall*	2/49	12/65	
7900	*Saint Peter's Hall*	4/49	12/64	
7901	*Dodington Hall*	3/49	2/64	
7902	*Eaton Mascot Hall*	3/49	6/64	
7903	*Foremarke Hall*	4/49	6/64	
7904	*Fountains Hall*	4/49	12/65	
7905	*Fowey Hall*	4/49	5/64	
7906	*Fron Hall*	12/49	3/65	
7907	*Hart Hall*	1/50	12/65	
7908	*Henshall Hall*	1/50	10/65	
7909	*Heveningham Hall*	1/50	11/65	
7910	*Hown Hall*	1/50	2/65	
7911	*Lady Margaret Hall*	2/50	12/63	
7912	*Little Linford Hall*	3/50	10/65	
7913	*Little Wyrley Hall*	3/50	3/65	
7914	*Lleweni Hall*	3/50	12/65	
7915	*Mere Hall*	3/50	10/65	
7916	*Mobberley Hall*	4/50	12/64	
7917	*North Aston Hall*	4/50	8/65	
7918	*Rhose Wood Hall*	4/50	2/65	
7919	*Runter Hall*	5/50	12/65	
7920	*Coney Hall*	9/50	6/65	
7921	*Edstone Hall*	9/50	12/63	
7922	*Salford Hall*	9/50	12/65	
7923	*Speke Hall*	9/50	6/65	
7924	*Thornycroft Hall*	9/50	12/65	
7925	*Westol Hall*	10/50	12/65	
7926	*Willey Hall*	10/50	12/64	
7927	*Willington Hall*	10/50	12/65	
7928	*Wolf Hall*	10/50	3/65	
7929	*Wyke Hall*	11/50	8/65	

'Grange' Class

No	Name	Date Built	Date Withdrawn	Notes
6800	*Arlington Grange*	8/36	6/64	
6801	*Aylburton Grange*	8/36	10/60	
6802	*Bampton Grange*	9/36	8/61	

No	Name	Date Built	Date Withdrawn	Notes
6803	Bucklebury Grange	9/36	9/65	
6804	Brockington Grange	9/36	8/64	
6805	Broughton Grange	9/36	3/61	
6806	Blackwell Grange	9/36	10/64	
6807	Birchwood Grange	9/36	12/63	7
6808	Beenham Grange	9/36	8/64	
6809	Burghclere Grange	9/36	7/63	
6810	Blakemere Grange	11/36	10/64	
6811	Cranbourne Grange	11/36	7/64	
6812	Chesford Grange	11/36	2/65	
6813	Eastbury Grange	12/36	9/65	
6814	Enborne Grange	12/36	12/63	
6815	Frilford Grange	12/36	11/65	
6816	Frankton Grange	12/36	7/65	
6817	Gwenddwr Grange	12/36	4/65	
6818	Hardwick Grange	12/36	4/64	
6819	Highnam Grange	12/36	11/65	
6820	Kingstone Grange	1/37	7/65	
6821	Leaton Grange	1/37	11/64	
6822	Manton Grange	1/37	9/64	
6823	Oakley Grange	1/37	6/65	
6824	Ashley Grange	1/37	4/64	
6825	Llanvair Grange	2/37	6/64	
6826	Nannerth Grange	2/37	5/65	
6827	Llanfrechfa Grange	2/37	9/65	
6828	Trellech Grange	2/37	7/63	
6829	Burmington Grange	3/37	11/65	
6830	Buckenhill Grange	8/37	10/65	
6831	Bearley Grange	8/37	10/65	
6832	Brockton Grange	8/37	1/64	
6833	Calcot Grange	8/37	10/65	
6834	Dummer Grange	8/37	6/64	7
6835	Eastham Grange	9/37	5/63	
6836	Estevarney Grange	9/37	8/65	
6837	Forthampton Grange	9/37	7/65	7
6838	Goodmoor Grange	9/37	11/65	7
6839	Hewell Grange	9/37	5/64	
6840	Hazeley Grange	9/37	2/65	
6841	Marlas Grange	9/37	6/65	
6842	Nunhold Grange	9/37	11/64	
6843	Poulton Grange	10/37	2/64	
6844	Penhydd Grange	10/37	4/64	
6845	Paviland Grange	10/37	9/64	
6846	Ruckley Grange	10/37	9/64	
6847	Tidmarsh Grange	10/37	12/65	
6848	Toddington Grange	10/37	12/65	
6849	Walton Grange	10/37	12/65	
6850	Cleeve Grange	10/37	12/64	
6851	Hurst Grange	11/37	8/65	7
6852	Headbourne Grange	11/37	1/64	
6853	Morehampton Grange	11/37	10/65	
6854	Roundhill Grange	11/37	9/65	
6855	Saighton Grange	11/37	10/65	
6856	Stowe Grange	11/37	11/65	
6857	Tudor Grange	11/37	10/65	
6858	Woolston Grange	12/37	10/65	
6859	Yiewsley Grange	12/37	11/65	
6860	Aberporth Grange	2/39	2/65	
6861	Crynant Grange	2/39	10/65	
6862	Derwent Grange	2/39	6/65	
6863	Dolhywel Grange	2/39	11/64	
6864	Dymock Grange	2/39	10/65	
6865	Hopton Grange	3/39	5/62	
6866	Morfa Grange	3/39	5/65	
6867	Peterston Grange	3/39	8/64	
6868	Penrhos Grange	3/39	10/65	
6869	Resolven Grange	3/39	7/65	
6870	Bodicote Grange	3/39	9/65	
6871	Bourton Grange	3/39	10/65	
6872	Crawley Grange	3/39	12/65	
6873	Caradoc Grange	4/39	6/64	
6874	Haughton Grange	4/39	9/65	
6875	Hindford Grange	4/39	3/64	
6876	Kingsland Grange	4/39	11/65	
6877	Llanfair Grange	4/39	3/65	
6878	Longford Grange	5/39	11/64	
6879	Overton Grange	5/39	10/65	

'Manor' Class

No	Name	Date Built	Date Withdrawn	Notes
7800	Torquay Manor	1/38	8/64	
7801	Anthony Manor	1/38	7/65	
7802	Bradley Manor	1/38	11/65	
7803	Barcote Manor	1/38	4/65	
7804	Baydon Manor	2/38	9/65	
7805	Broome Manor	3/38	12/64	
7806	Cockington Manor	3/38	11/64	
7807	Compton Manor	3/38	11/64	
7808	Cookham Manor	3/38	12/65	
7809	Childrey Manor	4/38	4/63	
7810	Draycott Manor	12/38	9/64	
7811	Dunley Manor	12/38	7/65	
7812	Erlestoke Manor	1/39	11/65	
7813	Freshford Manor	1/39	5/65	
7814	Fringford Manor	1/39	9/65	
7815	Fritwell Manor	1/39	10/64	
7816	Frilsham Manor	1/39	11/65	
7817	Garsington Manor	1/39	6/64	
7818	Granville Manor	1/39	1/65	
7819	Hinton Manor	2/39	11/65	
7820	Dinmore Manor	11/50	11/65	
7821	Ditcheat Manor	11/50	11/65	
7822	Foxcote Manor	12/50	11/65	
7823	Hook Norton Manor	12/50	7/64	
7824	Iford Manor	12/50	11/64	
7825	Lechlade Manor	12/50	5/64	
7826	Longworth Manor	12/50	4/65	
7827	Lydham Manor	12/50	10/65	
7828	Odney Manor	12/50	10/65	
7829	Ramsbury Manor	12/50	12/65	

Notes:

1 4972 was *St Brides Hall* when built
2 4985 was Allersley Hall until 3/31
3 5912 was Queens Hall until 5/35
4 Entered service without names
5 Rebuilt from 'Saint' class No 2925, renumbered 12/28
6 Received a direct hit from a German bomb on 29/4/41 and condemned at Swindon on 10/6/41
7 Later fitted with 3-row superheater boilers ('AK')

2
Trends in Mileages and Costs

The costs given below are taken from a number of sources and are in some cases averaged or include an estimated cost for the tender; they are, however, close to the 'real' figure for an engine in the relevant lot. Tenders were costed separately by the GWR but included by BR in locomotive costs. The accountants 'figures', however always included a cost for the tender which was 'written off' with the engine on withdrawal even though the tender, which had a life of its own was not in fact withdrawn.

The mileages are averages from the known mileages of locos in each lot and rounded to the nearest 1,000. Only the 'Halls' of lot 254 and some of lot 268 saw out their full life and nearly all the

'Halls', 'Granges', and 'Manors' saw their potential mileage unrealised due to their premature withdrawal in the 1960s. Inevitably the newer engines, with the lower mileages had cost more to build.

Cost per ton of empty weight for GW design mixed traffic engines in the late 1940s, were typically: 'County' class £109, 'Hall' class £106 and 'Manor' class £122. For comparison the light pacifics of O.V.S. Bulleid were £207 per ton (£19,557 each), with yet more expensive rebuildings costs to come and a running thermal efficiency less than any of the Churchward family of engines.

Lot No	Running Nos	Average cost per engine (with tender) £	Average mileage per engine[5]
'Halls'			
–	4900[1]	3150[2]	2,092,500[3]
254	4901-80	5383	1,302,000
268	4981-99, 5900	5355	1,213,000
275	5901-20	5259	1,201,000
281	5921-40	5165	1,181,000
290	5941-50	6129	1,077,000
297	5951-65	4946	1,037,000
304	5966-75	5048	972,000
311	5976-85	5400	894,000
327	5986-95	5410	828,000[4]
333	5996-99, 6900-5	5661	852,000
338	6906-15	6091	842,000
340	6916-58	6843	793,000
350	6959-70	8273	771,000
366	6971-90	9776	628,000
368	6991-99, 7900-19	10,596	567,000
376	7920-29	11,107	482,000

Lot No	Running Nos	Average cost per engine (with tender) £	Average mileage per engine[5]
'Granges'			
308	6800-79	4946	904,000
'Manors'			
316	7800-19	4944	806,000
377	7820-29	10,425	419,000

Notes

1 Originally No 2925.
2 Cost of rebuilding (engine only), original cost £2,726 (engine only).
3 Includes mileage as a 'Saint'.
4 Only small sample for this lot.
5 Mileages for engines running after December 1963 unknown. Therefore all figures on the low side.

3
Weight Diagrams

It should be noted that issued diagrams sometimes show non-existent types (eg engine and tender combinations known not to have existed). Many important modifications were not covered by a new diagram (eg 'Granges' with 3-row superheaters), in other cases minute detail changes appear on a new diagram. Thus the criteria for the issue of a new diagram is unknown. At least one case of a new diagram being issued to the same letter as a previous one has been traced. Below are listed the two-cylinder 4-6-0 diagrams; this style of diagram appeared before the letter classification, No 100 as built therefore, is unlettered as it was rebuilt before the new nomenclature was used.

Below:
Near the end, a rundown 'Hall' No 6953 without nameplates at Southall shed on 8 August 1965. *R. C. Riley*

Diagram No	Description
4-6-0	
–	No 100, as built
C	No 100, as reboilered in 1903
D	No 98, as built
E	Nos 173-178
F	Nos. 2902-10, as built with short cone boilers
G	No 2901 Schmidt superheater 18⅜in dia cyls
I	Nos.2911-30 as built
L	No 2922, Swindon No 2 superheater
O	No 2913, Swindon No 3 superheater
P	No 100, superheated
R	Nos.2931-40 as built
V	29xx class, 18½in cylinders
X	No 2925 rebuilt to ''Hall'' class
A^1	4901 class, 3,500gal tender (Churchward type)
A^2	4901 class, 3,500gal tender (Collett type)
A^3	4901 class, 4,000gal tender
A^4	No 2935 with R. C. Poppet valve gear.
A^8	68xx class, 3,500gal tender (Churchward type)
A^9	78xx class
A^{14}	6959 class, 3-row superheater
A^{15}	6959 class, 2-row superheater
A^{16}	1000 class, as built
A^{17}	No 1000, experimental double chimney
A^{21}	39xx class, oil-burning
A^{25}	6959 class, Hawksworth SS tender
A^{27}	1000 class, double chimney
A^{28}	68xx class, 4,000gal tender
A^{31}	4901 class, 3-row superheater

Weights of engines The following are official weights in working order of the 2-cylinder 4-6-0 classes.

Bogie	Leading Coupled	Driving	Trailing Coupled	Engine Total	Diagrams	Notes
15t 6c	17t 10c	18t 0c	17t 0c	67t 16c	C, P	No 100, as built and rebuilt.
16t 8c	16t 8c	18t 0c	17t 10c	68t 6c	D	No 98, as built.
16t 0c	18t 0c	18t 4c	18t 0c	70t 4c	?	No 171, as built.
16t 0c	19t 10c	19t 10c	15t 10c	70t 10c	4-4-2B, F	LOT 154 and No 171 as 4-4-2.
16t 12c	18t 0c	18t 12c	18t 10c	71t 14c	E	LOT 154, engines built as 4-6-0.
17t 4c	18t 0c	18t 8c	18t 8c	72t 0c	F,G,I,L,O,R,V	All 'Ladies', 'Saints' and 'Courts' etc.
19t 8c	18t 6c	18t 12c	18t 14c	75t 0c	A^4	No 2953 with R.C. valve gear.
17t 12c	18t 0c	18t 9c	18t 9c	72t 10c	X	No 2925 rebuilt to 'Hall'.
18t 10c	18t 12c	18t 19c	18t 19c	75t 0c	A^1,A^2,A^3,A^{31}	4901 class, 'Halls'.
18t 10c	18t 15c	19t 3c	19t 3c	75t 11c	A^{21}	39xx class, oil burning.
18t 6c	19t 0c	19t 5c	19t 5c	75t 16c	A^{14},A^{25}	6959 class, 'Modified Halls'.
18t 1c	19t 2c	19t 2c	19t 2c	75t 7c	A^{15}	6959 class, with 2-row superheater.
18t 16c	18t 8c	18t 8c	18t 8c	74t 0c	A^8	68xx class, 'Granges'.
18t 10c	17t 5c	17t 1c	16t 2c	68t 18c	A^9	78xx class, 'Manors'.
17t 15c	19t 14c	19t 14c	19t 14c	76t 17c	A^{16},A^{17},A^{27}	10xx class, 'Counties'.

4
Dimensions

Class:	6959	68xx	78xx
Diagram:	A25	A8	A9
Cylinders:	18½×30in	18½×30in	18×30in
Motion:	Stephenson	Stephenson	Stephenson
Valves:	10in P.V.	9in P.V.	10in P.V.
Driving wheels:	6ft 0in	5ft 8in	5ft 8in
Tractive effort (85%):	27,275lb	28,875lb	27,340lb
Adhesion weight:	57t. 10c.	55t. 4c.	50t. 8c.
Factor of adhesion:	4·72	4·28	4·13
Boiler Type:	No. 1	No. 1	No. 14
Prefix:	AK	AH	ZA
Maximum diameter:	5ft 6in	5ft 6in	5ft 3in
Minimum diameter:	4ft 10¹³⁄₁₆in	4ft 10¹³⁄₁₆in	4ft 7⅝in
Length between tubeplates:	15ft 2⁷⁄₁₆in	15ft 2⁷⁄₁₆in	13ft 0⁵⁄₁₆in
Small tubes – Number:	145	176	158
External diameter:	2in	2in	2in
Large tubes – Number:	21	14	12
External diameter:	5⅛in	5⅛in	5⅛in
Superheater – Type:	3-Row	2-Row	2-Row
Units:	Melesco	6-Tube	6-Tube
Number of elements:	84	84	72
Diameter of elements:	1¼in	1in	1in
Length:	14ft 2in	14ft 11in	13ft 0in
Heating Surfaces – Firebox:	154·9sq ft	154·78sq ft	140·0sq ft
Tubes:	1582·6sq ft	1686·6sq ft	1285·5sq ft
Total evaporative:	1737·5sq ft	1841·38sq ft	1425·5sq ft
Superheater:	295sq ft	253·38sq ft	160sq ft
Area of firegrate:	27·07sq ft	27·07sq ft	22·1sq ft
Boiler pressure:	225lb/sq in	225lb/sq in	225lb/sq in

Left:
Short turntables could cause problems, here solved by the use of outriggers. No 7808 *Cookham Manor* on an SLS special at Ludgershall on the MSWJ on 10 September 1961.
R. E. James-Robertson

5
Valve Events

The valve dimensions of some two-cyclinder 4-6-0 classes is given below; it can be clearly seen that there was a considerable increase in maximum valve travel over the years.

Tables of valve events for Great Western locomotives were as rare in Swindon Works as outside! The following table for 'Modified Hall' No 7916 was constructed from measurements taken when the locomotive was tested on the stationary plant and on the road in 1951.

Class	Port width	Lap	Lead*	Max travel
No 98	1¾	1½	³⁄₁₆	5⅞
2901	1¾	1⅝	⅛	6¼
4901	2⅛	1¾	³⁄₁₆	7
1000	2¼	1⅞	³⁄₁₆	7¼
* In running cut-off				

TABLE OF VALVE EVENTS, ENGINE No 7916

Piston Stroke 30in; Steam Lap = 1¾in; Exhaust Lap = 0in

FORWARD GEAR

Nominal Cut-Off %	Travel of Valve (in)	Lead F.S. (in)	Lead B.S. (in)	Opening to steam F.S. (in)	Opening to steam B.S. (in)	Steam Cut-Off % F.S.	Steam Cut-Off % B.S.	Exhaust Opens % F.S.	Exhaust Opens % B.S.	Exhaust Closes % F.S.	Exhaust Closes % B.S.
Full Gear	6.91	−.17	−.19	1.65	1.76	77.2	77.7	94.2	93.7	94.2	93.7
75	6.75	−.14	−.17	1.58	1.68	75.9	76.4	93.5	93.3	93.5	93.3
70	6.29	−.09	−.11	1.36	1.43	72.2	72.8	91.9	91.9	91.9	91.9
60	5.58	−.01	−.03	1.02	1.06	63.4	64.9	88.7	89.0	88.7	89.0
50	4.99	+.06	+.04	.71	.73	51.6	54.4	83.9	84.7	83.9	84.7
40	4.57	+.1	+.09	.53	.54	40.2	43.6	79.3	80.6	79.3	80.6
30	4.28	+.13	+.12	.39	.39	29.4	32.7	73.6	75.6	73.6	75.6
25	4.15	+.14	+.13	.33	.32	24.7	27.9	71.0	72.9	71.0	72.9
20	4.05	+.16	+.14	.28	.27	19.3	21.8	67.5	69.3	67.5	69.3
15	3.97	+.16	+.15	.24	.23	15.5	17.3	64.1	66.1	64.1	66.1
Mid-Gear	3.83	+.18	+.15	.18	.15	6.0	6.1				

BACKWARD GEAR

Nominal Cut-Off %	Travel of Valve (in)	Lead F.S. (in)	Lead B.S. (in)	Opening to steam F.S. (in)	Opening to steam B.S. (in)	Steam Cut-Off % F.S.	Steam Cut-Off % B.S.	Exhaust Opens % F.S.	Exhaust Opens % B.S.	Exhaust Closes % F.S.	Exhaust Closes % B.S.
Full Gear	6.62	−.19	−.17	1.62	1.5	78.3	77.8	94.6	94.0	94.6	94.0
75	6.42	−.15	−.15	1.5	1.42	76.4	76.0	94.0	93.8	94.0	93.8
70	5.99	−.08	−.09	1.28	1.21	71.7	71.6	92.5	92.3	92.5	92.3
60	5.3	+.02	0	.92	.88	61.6	61.5	88.9	88.4	88.9	88.4
50	4.81	+.08	+.06	.68	.63	49.5	50.8	84.9	84.4	84.9	84.4
40	4.45	+.13	+.1	.48	.47	36.9	38.6	79.6	79.6	79.6	79.6
30	4.18	+.16	+.14	.35	.33	28.6	28.0	74.1	74.3	74.1	74.3
25	4.08	+.17	+.15	.3	.28	21.0	22.7	70.4	70.6	79.4	70.6
20	4.0	+.17	+.15	.27	.23	17.3	18.5	67.1	67.6	67.1	67.6
15	3.94	+.19	+.15	.24	.2	13.1	14.0	62.9	63.7	62.9	63.7
Mid-Gear	3.86	+.19	+.17	.19	.17	6.1	6.2				

Note: F.S. = Front Stroke; B.S. = Back Stroke.
Front Stroke is the Piston moving from Front towards Firebox.

6
Churchward and Superheating

In 1914 Churchward prepared a report 'on the question of economic production and use of steam on locomotives' – Subject V for discussion at the Ninth Congress of the International Railway Association. Due to the war this report wasn't published until 1921 (IRC *Bulletin* Vol III No 10) and an additional section was prepared to bring the subject up to date. Below is reproduced the table of railway companies and their superheater engines followed by the 1921 supplement. The vigour with which Churchward went to the task is convincingly demonstrated. Goethe had an appropriate saying for Churchward and the superheater controversy. 'Die Tat is Alles, nicht der Ruhm' (The deed is everything, its repute nothing).

1914 Table		**BRITISH**				
		Superheater engines			Non-superheater engines	
ADMINISTRATION	In 1910	Present time Including conversions	On order		Since 1910	On order
Great Western Railway	29	801[1]	85		–	–
London & North Western Railway	–	158	93		107	–
Midland Railway	–	62[1]	31		–	–
Great Eastern Railway	–	37	23		85	6
Great Central Railway	1	142[2]	–		–	–
Lancashire & Yorkshire Railway	27	87	68		50	–
Caledonian Railway	5	33	9		51	(including those on order).
North Staffordshire Railway	–	8	8			Not stated
Furness Railway	5	13	–		–	–
	67	1,341	317		293	6
		1,658			299	

[1] Includes one compound locomotive HP steam only superheated.
[2] Includes two compound locomotives HP steam only superheated.

Above:
A batch of 4-6-0s were built in 1906 and named after 'Ladies'. The first No 2901 *Lady Superior* was built with a Schmidt superheater, **the first modern superheater locomotive to run in Britain. The third engine *Lady of Lyons,* shown here while being run-in light engine, achieved a speed around 120mph.** *Real Photos (18160)*

AMERICAN AND CANADIAN

ADMINISTRATION	Superheater engines			Non-superheater engines	
	In 1910	Present time Including conversions	On order	Since 1910	On order
Chicago, Burlington & Quincy	–	286 (11 comp; 1 Mallet)	– (6 switch and	7 Mallet comp)	–
Delaware, Lackawanna & Western	2	70	34	42	Not stated
Erie	–	122	20	30 (Switchers)	–
Pennsylvania	–	251 (1 compound)	1,281	Not stated	All sincee 1911 superheated
Chicago & Alton	–	60	–	Not stated	
El Paso & South Western	–	26	–	–	
Central Vermont	–	–	–	–	
Missourie Pacific	–	73	37	–	
Central of New Jersey	–	14	–	22	–
Boston & Albany	–	33 (4 compound HP only)	–	–	–
Southern of Washington	–	85 (2 compound)	–	110	–
Elgin, Joliet & Eastern	–	21	–	Not stated	
Chicago, Rock Island & Pacific	9	109	55	–	–
Delaware & Hudson River	–	27	–	–	
Chicago, Indianapolis & Louisville	–	30	–	–	
Grand Trunk	–	94 (1 compound)	–	–	
Grand Rapids & Indiana	Not stated	–	–	–	
Mobile & Ohio	–	9	–	–	–
Atchison, Topeka & Santa Fe	–	55 (25 compound)	54	No definite reply	
Missouri, Kansas & Texas	–	57	40	Not stated	
Pennsylvania Lines West of Pittsburgh	–	66	140	50	–
Norfolk & Western	5 (H&L all comp)	64 (46 comp)	49 (44 comp)	Not stated	
Baltimore & Ohio	–	134 (20 comp)	150 (10 comp)	35	
Queen & Crescent	–	47	Not stated	5	–
Quebec Central of Canada	29	34	–	2	–
Vandalia	–	4	Not stated	Not stated	
Atlanta & West Point	–	1	–	2	–
Cleveland, Cincinnati, Chicago & St Louis	–	198	20	35	–
	45	1,970	1,880	659	–
			3,850		

EMPIRE OF INDIA AND OTHERS

ADMINISTRATION	Superheater engines			Non-superheater engines	
	In 1910	Present time	On order	Since 1910	On order
Bengal & Nagpur	–	–	10	43	–
South Indian	–	2	13	Not stated	
North Western of India	–	2	9		–
Eastern Bengal	–	–	44		–
Oudh & Rohilkhand	–	3	8		–
Great Indian Peninsula	–	–	–		–
Bombay Baroda (Metre gauge)	–	1	3		–
Bombay Baroda (B-gauge)	–	13	29		
				Not intended to fit	
East Indian	–	–	–	Superheaters	
Madras & Southern Mahratta	–	4	–	Not stated	
Buenos Ayres Western	4	24	20	6 shunting tanks	
Argentine State Railways	–	1	–	Not stated	
South African Railways	3	49	110	72	–
	7	99	246	121	
				345	

BRITISH

1921 Table

ADMINISTRATION	Superheater engines			Non-superheater engines	
	In 1910	Present time Including conversions	On order	Since 1910	On order
Great Western Railway[1]	29	1,472	170	Nil	Nil
London & North Western Railway	–	613	111	–	–
Midland Railway[2]	–	257 (9 compound)	111 (6 compound)	–	–
Great Eastern Railway	–	178	19	101	15
Great Central Railway	–	373 (2 compound)	50	–	–
Lancashire & Yorkshire Railway	27	249	39	50	–
Caledonian Railway	5	103	14	51	–
London, Brighton & South Coast Railway	15	50	5	10	–
London & South Western Railway[5]	–	86	31	Not stated	–

AMERICAN AND CANADIAN

	In 1910	Present time	On order	Since 1910	On order
Erie	–	552	–	–	–
Pennsylvania	–	3,399 (10 compound)	–	Nil	–
Chicago, Rock Island & Pacific	4	417	–	–	–
Grand Trunk	–	351	–	–	–
Atchison, Topeka & Santa Fe[3]	–	–	–	–	–
Norfolk & Western	–	408 (268 compound)	–	–	–
Baltimore & Ohio[4]	–	738	–	354	–
Cleveland, Cincinnati, Chicago & St Louis	–	628	9	35	–

No replies have been received from other administrations previously shown

[1] Superheater engines in service include four compound locos. HP steam only superheated.
[2] Superheater engines shown on order include 91 saturated engines being rebuilt as superheaters.
[3] No figures for 1921.
[4] 202 of the 354 non-superheaters have since been fitted with superheaters and are included in the second column.
[5] No non-superheater engines have been introduced since 1914.

Index